Talking About Yourself

Talking About Yourself

What You Didn't Learn in College About Job Interviews

Emily Messersmith

Charles Burhans

ISBN 978-1534714786

Cover design by Zeke Burhans

Contents

We've designed this book for young adults who are transitioning from college into the professional workforce. (By "college," we mean any kind of post-high school education, including technical schools, business schools, universities, and the like.) As a recent or soon-to-be college graduate, or someone who has decided now isn't the right time to stay in college, you're at a unique time in your professional development. You've thought about your interests and skills—what makes you happy and where you, as an individual, excel. You may have identified a field in which you'd like to spend a good part of your future career. Perhaps you've even had the opportunity to volunteer or intern in that field. But you probably don't have much professional experience. And even if you do have a little experience in your desired field, you probably need to draw upon experiences other than paid work or internships—experiences like extracurricular activities, college classes, and volunteer work—to prove what you know and can do. The purpose of this book is to show you how to communicate these experiences and interests—how to talk about yourself—to potential employers.

Our experience and research has led us to develop a way of thinking about the job interview that is distinct from the advice that appears in other books and websites. We don't think it's particularly helpful to memorize answers to common questions, for instance, or to think of yourself as a good fit for any organization that might hire you, or to attempt to exude raw confidence. In the chapters that follow, we stress instead the importance of understanding the needs and interests of the people who will interview you and evaluating not simply the needs of the organization but your relationship to those needs. Most importantly, we teach you how to tell your story in a way that interviewers will understand and appreciate.

Because this book is focused on the experiences and needs of people who are currently enrolled in or who have recently left college, many of the examples in the pages that follow involve people who are at the beginning of their careers. Nevertheless, we believe that the core advice in this book holds for everyone. No matter your field or the nature of your experience, this book will help you to tell your story and land you the job that you deserve.

To get the most out of this book, you'll want to work through the activities we have included in several of the chapters. Copies of the worksheets necessary for these activities are available on our website, morethananswers.com.

CHAPTER 1: OUR STORY

When we set out to learn about the interview process, we'd had many job interviews, both successful and unsuccessful. We had also interviewed many people, including large numbers of recent graduates. Our experiences on both sides of the process made us curious to know more. How do most employers understand the interview process? How do they communicate their needs to the people whom they interview? What common approaches do job seekers take when they interview? How do people who interview well communicate with their potential employers? Do these methods work everywhere and at all times? We directed these questions toward one overarching goal: helping people find jobs in which they are satisfied, useful, and successful.

Like most people, we brought certain common sense assumptions to our first job interviews. Emily had her first interview at the age of fourteen. She was a short, shy girl with long blond hair. She doesn't remember what she wore, but does remember anxiously tapping her foot on a linoleum floor as she waited for her interview. She'd heard that her interviewers would ask questions, but what type of questions would they ask? Should she shake hands? Curtsy?

The interview took place in a non-descript office building. When her name was called, Emily walked into a big room that seemed too big even for the long plastic table and the six grown-ups seated there. She took an open seat at the far end of the table, smiled, and introduced herself, just as her mom had said to do. The grown-ups asked her about her school grades, to subtract in her head, and to talk about her plans for the summer. They asked about the sorts of things she liked and the sorts of things she didn't. She wasn't sure why they were asking these questions, but she wanted the grown-ups to like her, so she answered their questions honestly with the first words that came into her mind. Was this what all interviews were like?

She must have done well enough, because that summer she worked as a desk attendant at her local swimming pool. She greeted people, made change when they wanted to buy swim goggles, and called someone in the concession stand if she had any questions. Mostly, she read magazines to pass the time.

We call Emily's method the *smile-and-be-nice* approach. It comes from a desire to be pleasant and develop rapport with an interviewer, often because the job seeker doesn't have a sense of what else the interviewer might be seeking out of the interaction. Unfortunately, it puts the onus on interviewers to intuit—often in a very short amount of time—the relevance of your experience, skills, and knowledge. It over-emphasizes likeability, and while it may get you a summer gig, it's rarely enough to win you a professional job.

Emily learned this the hard way. Several years later, in college, she wanted to upgrade the tips she earned as a waitress at a local diner by working at a higher price-per-plate restaurant, an Olive Garden. She went to her interview with a winning smile and a good attitude, but this time the interviewer was looking for something else. Reflecting on the interview, she thinks the interviewer didn't just want to hire a good waitress; he wanted a good waitress who would fit at the Olive Garden. She hadn't known there was a difference.

After graduating, Emily went to graduate school and obtained a doctorate in education and psychology. She studied how teenagers and young adults think about and prepare for their careers. She examined factors that can get in the way of young adults reaching their goals, like having conflicting goals that are hard to reach simultaneously, or feeling out of place in college classrooms.

As a graduate student, Emily found herself on the other side of the table, conducting interviews and hiring students to help code data and perform literature reviews. It became clear very quickly that the smile-and-be-nice approach is quite common.

She saw still more of this approach a few years later, when she began interviewing potential employees for the nonprofit research organization where she was employed. She would carefully analyze resumes, think deeply about the sort of employee her organization needed, and compose a long list of questions, but the people whom she interviewed rarely seemed to have prepared beyond submitting letters, dressing nicely, and stepping into the room. Many of these people were clearly polite and even well qualified, but they struggled to communicate their goals, interests, and fit for the organization.

As someone who interviewed prospective employees, Emily also spoke with many job seekers who took a *this-is-me* approach to the interview. These candidates seemed to think that it's absolutely essential to be yourself during an interview. This is an appealing approach, because it is indeed important to be true to yourself, but these candidates also seemed to forget that their answers were being evaluated. They told their entire life stories freely, as if they were on reality TV rather than at a job interview. These candidates were very easy to get to know, so easy in fact, that Emily quickly learned all of the reasons they might not make great hires.

A successful interview is almost always a matter of preparation. Sometimes people don't prepare because they don't understand that it will greatly help their chances of being hired. Others don't know how to prepare or don't think they can spare the time it takes. Sometimes, people fail to prepare because they are afraid of becoming emotionally invested in being hired and fear the pain of rejection. Regardless, preparation often makes the difference between a polite rejection and a good job offer.

Nevertheless, preparation itself doesn't ensure a good interview. Emily interviewed other people who seemed to have prepared answers as if they were taking a test. They made assumptions about what the interviewer wanted to hear, but too often they got this wrong. What's worse, these candidates often seemed willing to exaggerate their abilities or overstate their involvement in past activities, just so that they could provide "correct" answers. We call this the *brown-noser* approach. These interviewees seemed to believe that interview questions have correct answers, and they seemed to think that if they delivered these correct answers, they would get the job.

Charles's experiences were similar. In his first job, he spent his summers stocking shelves and working the cash register at his aunt's lakeside convenience store. Later, as a teenager, he wanted a job that he could do after school and on weekends. The local Walmart was hiring, and as a student with great grades, perfect attendance, and several years of retail experience, he figured that he was a shoo-in for a position as a sales associate. His confidence was further bolstered when he was immediately invited for an interview. He arrived on time, ready to talk about his experience. But he wasn't ready when the interviewer asked him a question unrelated to his work experience. "Why do you want to work for Walmart?" Charles answered honestly: "Because I need a job."

Much to his surprise, Charles wasn't hired. Looking back, he now knows that one of the things Walmart was looking for in its entry-level associates (probably all of its employees) was an interest in working at Walmart. In all likelihood, if Charles had shown real enthusiasm, he would have been offered the job. Instead he came off sounding self-centered and disinterested. We call this the *obviously-strong-candidate* approach. It over-emphasizes skills and experience, with the assumption that the most qualified candidate is the best one. People who take this approach often come across as unenthusiastic during the interview. They fail to realize that the people who interview don't stand in their shoes. Interviewers need a way to imagine why it makes sense to hire *you*, not just your skills.

Charles learned from this episode. He realized that if being smart, articulate, and experienced isn't enough for Walmart, it probably isn't enough for any other job. He started to think more about the social contract that exists between employers and employees. In most organizations, employers want good things for their employees. They want to pay fair wages, have happy and satisfied workers, and provide opportunities for their employees to learn, grow, and advance. In return, they expect a few things, things that are hardly unreasonable. Employers expect that their employees will work diligently, look for ways that they and the larger organization might improve, and contribute to a pleasant workplace. Charles realized that if he wanted a good job and a meaningful career, he was going to have to learn how to demonstrate to an interviewer that he understood this give-and-take.

After graduating from college, Charles found himself working for a small organization. He became heavily involved in all aspects of human resources, despite the fact that he is an engineer by both education and training. Sitting through interviews for jobs at all levels of the organization, he found himself questioning why it was so hard to get job seekers to tell him what he wanted to know. Those experiences made it abundantly clear to him that job seekers can take a few simple steps in order to improve their chances of landing good jobs and meaningful careers.

One step is just to put in a little effort preparing for an interview. Some candidates take what we call a *deer-in-headlights* approach by doing nothing but showing up at (or near) the scheduled time. They got stumped when Charles asked what should have been easy questions about previous jobs. Worse, they often didn't recall simple facts about their own resumes.

Our experiences have showed us that many people are unprepared for and ill-advised about the interview process. Together, we decided that we wanted to understand the nature of these misconceptions as well as the most successful methods for interview preparation and performance. We read books, research articles, and Internet resources designed to teach people how to interview and be interviewed. We drew upon psychological and career development theories and upon Emily's doctoral and post-doctoral research. We spent hours and hours talking to hiring managers about how they hire and what they expect from job candidates, and we've now spent many more hours helping job seekers learn how to be hired.

But we didn't stop there. We also wanted to add a systematic analysis of people's actual experiences to this conversation about the interview process, so we advertised for people who were looking for jobs and who wanted to learn more about interviewing. We offered to give them a mock interview, with feedback, in exchange for filming the session. (Where we've quoted these interviews, we used pseudonyms and edited for clarity.)

What we learned from these mock interviews was fascinating. We discovered that there are all sorts of nasty rumors out there that interfere with interview preparation and performance. We also learned that job seekers frequently communicate in ways that confuse the people who interview them. They often unconsciously offer their interviewers a set of facts that fail to create a coherent picture, or story, of their past experience and present fit for the job in question. Why do they do this? These facts usually make sense to job seekers themselves, who are, after all, reflecting upon their own lives, but they don't yet constitute a story that might make sense to others. The upshot is that while job seekers usually believe that they will be a good employee, they often don't know how to convince a hiring manager of that fact.

This book is based on both our experiences hiring employees and our research on how people commonly, and all too often mistakenly, approach the job interview. What is important—more than being likable, more than studying the "correct" answers, more than letting your experience speak for itself—is that you learn why certain ways of responding to the interview setting are more likely to lead to a job offer. As we will demonstrate in the chapters that follow, this involves learning strategies that will help you to improve your interviewing skills in general, but it will also involve understanding which answers are best *for you*. Interviews do not proceed randomly; you have the power to influence the outcome of an interview through the way you act, what you say, and how you say it.

CHAPTER 2: THE POINT OF THE JOB INTERVIEW

Before every mock interview session that we filmed, we asked our job seekers, *What do you think interviewers are looking for?* A full sixty percent of this group spontaneously said that interviewers are looking for one of two things, a confident person or a likable person. Often, our interviewees thought that interviewers were looking for both qualities. The number of job seekers who think confidence and likability are the most important things to convey to potential employers isn't all that surprising. This advice regularly appears online, in books, and even from the mouths of some career coaches.

For many people, the idea that interviewers prize confidence and likability over all other qualities is disconcerting. After all, most of us think of these traits as natural, or inherent, qualities of individual personalities, and we don't have much control over the basic nature of our personalities. Especially not in the few short days leading up to a job interview.

We cannot stress this enough: demonstrating your confidence and likability is *not* the point of an interview. In fact, focusing on appearing confident and friendly can actually be detrimental to your prospects, especially if you haven't already mastered the other elements of a good interview. We believe that it's better to focus on aspects of the interview that you can control and develop.

Remember Emily's inability to convince the manager at Olive Garden to hire her? Charles's miserable attempt to be hired at his local Walmart? Like most people, we misunderstood the nature of the process when we interviewed for these jobs. The point of a job interview is not to wow your potential boss with your confidence or charm. It's not even to make plain your wonderful years of relevant experience. *The point of a job interview is to give your potential employer and you a chance to evaluate your appropriateness for the job.*

Why is this the case? When both you and the interviewer make accurate assessments of your suitability for the other, each of you maximizes the possibility of a good match. A good match means that your employer will be satisfied by your productivity and, even more importantly, that you will be satisfied with your work. As we'll stress below, you do *not* want a job for which you are a bad match.

So is confidence a bad thing? No. Good interviewers understand the point of the interview process, and they will usually forgive you if you're not perfectly confident. They may, however, want you to demonstrate that you can do the job effectively. When an employer says they're looking for confidence, it rarely means that they're looking for someone whose voice doesn't waiver, whose palms don't get sweaty, or whose posture exudes real power. It means they're looking for someone who knows that they can do the job for which they applied and do it really well. You can show this kind of confidence while your leg is jittering under the table. Confidence during the interview is *not* the same as confidence in your ability to do the job.

YOUR TWO RESPONSIBILITIES

Rather than think of the interview as a chance to display confidence and likability, it's better to keep in mind two responsibilities. If you can master these, confidence and likability will take care of themselves. Have you ever played the game Two Truths and a Lie? It's the one where you tell a group of strangers (or friends at a party) two things that are true about you and one thing that's a lie. They then guess which one is the lie.

Let's play that game with facts about job interviews. Which one of these is a myth?

- You should try to make the interviewer feel comfortable hiring you.
- You should evaluate the organization during the interview.
- You should convince the interviewer that you're the best candidate for the job.

Most people think that all of these statements are true. But this isn't a trick question. Only the first two are true. Because this is so counterintuitive, let's go over each statement in turn.

You *do* need to try to make the interviewer feel comfortable hiring you. This comfort will come naturally from their belief that you can do the job, that you want to do the job, and that you won't create problems in the office.

You should also use the interview as an opportunity to evaluate the organization. There are several components of this evaluation. You should think about whether you:

- Want this job at all,
- Can succeed in it,
- Want to work with this particular boss, and
- Want to work for this particular organization.

We recognize that this may sound naïve, particularly if jobs are not plentiful in your field. But the fact remains that you are much more likely to be satisfied in a job, succeed in it, and to succeed more quickly, if the job matches your talents and needs. In our experience, far too many people are afraid to mess up their chances of being the person who gets an offer. By failing to ask questions about things that are important to them and then accepting any offer that comes their way, they sometimes find themselves in positions that don't match their long-term goals. They don't spend any time after the interview thinking about how it went and whether the position is indeed a good match to their specific talents and needs.

We come now to our myth: it is *not* your responsibility to make the interviewer think you are the best candidate for the job. Why not? Frankly, this is out of your hands. You have no idea who else applied for the job, let alone how well the other candidates might match the position.

In fact, if you are not the best person for the job but you do somehow manage to convince an interviewer that you are, you would be creating much more harm than good. You would be relying on the interviewer to make an important decision for you. Not all interviewers are good at choosing the right person to hire. Why would you want to leave your life in their hands? The organization and its employees would find themselves with a second-tier colleague, and you would be putting yourself into a position that you may not like all that much—or worse, one that demands more than you can deliver. Why would you want all of that?

Take Jeremy for instance. Before he came to talk to us, he had been miserable in a job as a retail sales supervisor. He had been promised a promotion when his boss left the company, but someone from the outside was hired instead. Even worse, his new boss's management style was to micromanage. As a seasoned supervisor, Jeremy hated his boss's approach of demanding daily, after-hours updates. He went on the job market and took the first job that was offered to him.

Unfortunately, Jeremy soon realized that he had jumped out of the frying pan and into the fire. He thought that his management experience with people would easily transfer to managing projects, but he was wrong. In his new job, the budgeting and time management procedures were very different from what he had done in the past, and his new employer expected him to hit the ground running. It quickly became clear to him that, even though he seemed qualified to succeed in this job, it wasn't the right position for him. He came home every day even more miserable than he had been in his last job. It would have been better for him to wait another few weeks and take a different job—one that he would be more satisfied with in the long run.

The fact that you aren't responsible for proving your absolute excellence is a good thing. It means that it's easier to tell a compelling story about your good qualities, and easier to be honest (though tactful) when describing the areas in which you hope to improve. It also means that you will be hired for jobs that you can actually do, and consequently, that your manager will have reasonable expectations for your first few months on the job. A perfect job interview doesn't require you to be perfect—it requires you to be prepared.

FURTHER MYTHS AND MISCONCEPTIONS

To reiterate, you have two central goals in any interview. You need to do your best to make your interviewer feel comfortable hiring you, and you should take the time to evaluate whether you want the position and like the organization. What's more, one of the most widely held beliefs about the point of a job interview—the idea that job candidates need to prove they are the candidate who should be hired—is actually a myth. Unfortunately, this is not the only myth that can damage your performance during an interview and weaken your chances of landing a great job. Let's go over a few more.

Myth: The best way to prepare for a job interview is to practice answering common interview questions.

Truth: Simply practicing answers won't make the *content* of your answers any better. As we'll describe in great detail in the chapters that follow, you need to have a coherent story before you decide how to answer particular questions. After you have your story, practicing answers will help you deliver this story in a compelling manner. A good story is more important than answers to specific questions.

For the time being, keep this as an interview mantra: *there are no "correct" answers*. This goes for questions about you, your experience, or your fit for the job. A good answer for you might be a bad answer coming from a different candidate. Even more interesting, a good answer in one of your interviews may be a bad answer in another.

Myth: You either ace an interview (and get a job offer) or fail (and don't get a job offer).

Truth: Getting a job offer after every interview doesn't necessarily mean that you've done well. In fact, it might mean you haven't communicated clearly. If you get midway through an interview and realize that the organization or the position isn't the right fit for you, you should let the interviewer know. (Maybe not right then, but you could let them know in a thank you note that you are no longer interested in the position.) Why waste your time going back for a second interview? Why waste the interviewer's time putting together an offer if you aren't going to accept it?

In addition, you can do a great job at the interview but just not be the best match for that particular organization. Rather than think in terms of scarcity—"I need this job, any job"—try to view this positively. Not receiving an offer does not mean that you've failed. It definitely does not mean that the interviewer thought that you weren't good enough, smart enough, or sufficiently likeable. On the contrary, it may very well mean that you succeeded in giving the interviewer the right information, information that allowed them to find an employee who is more suitable for that particular position, and information that now allows you to move on and find a better match for your future.

Interviewing is not a zero-sum game; you don't win or lose. You either find a job that is a great match for your needs and talents, or you discover that this particular job was not a good match.

Myth: A good resume and cover letter communicate to the interviewer everything that they need to know.

Truth: Despite all of the hard work you have put into your resume and letter, they are only brief abstracts of your experience. If your life was a novel, could it be told in one page? Interviewers need to know about your experience and education, but they also want to see how you communicate and whether you are able to present yourself professionally. What's more, a single line about your college major or last summer's internship will hardly tell them everything they need to know about your experience. You'll need to provide much more detail during the interview itself. Think of it this way: your resume and cover letter are conversation starters.

Myth: If you are offered a job, you should take it.

Truth: Your parents (or your rent bill) may tell you otherwise, but you don't actually want every job. Before you accept a job offer, you need to evaluate its terms, the manager under whom you'll be working, and the nature of the organization itself in order to decide whether the job is a good fit. When you fit a particular job, you appreciate the mission of the organization and you're able to work well with your coworkers. It's better to have a significant gap in your work history than to accept a job at a company that everyone knows to be a pyramid scheme. In fact, that's the kind of job that could actually hurt your prospects later on, were it to appear on your resume. Future hiring managers may interpret a stint at a company with a negative reputation as an indication of poor judgment or as enculturation in ineffective business practices.

Be realistic, of course. You may not be able to wait for the job of your dreams, but you certainly needn't take a job just because it was offered to you. By taking a passive role in your job search and jumping at the first offer, you risk wasting several months of your life in a stressful job before hopping right back into the job market. Instead, take the time to evaluate the interviewer, the office culture, and your overall interview experience. Make sure that you are excited about the new role before you agree to take it on. A good job doesn't merely satisfy a need for money; a good job has deeper meaning. Fulfill your responsibility to yourself by making sure you get something worthwhile out of your next job.

Myth: If someone has multiple interviews and no job offers, they are most likely unemployable.

Truth: If you were truly unemployable, you wouldn't be reading this book. Just as all interviews shouldn't lead to job offers, an absence of job offers does not mean that you're doomed to a life as a ditch digger. Even experienced job seekers can improve their interview skills. Going through multiple interviews without an offer means a few *good* things: you have a resume and cover letter that employers find compelling, hiring managers believe that you meet their basic qualifications, and companies have considered hiring you. Those are already major accomplishments.

A lack of job offers is usually a symptom of other things than raw employability. It may mean that there is very strong competition for the jobs you're seeking, that interviewers are finding red flags in some of your answers (more on that later), or that the jobs you're applying for don't quite line up with your skills. All of these things are fixable.

Myth: Interviewers often try to induce stress and discomfort.

Truth: You will rarely, if ever, encounter a psychopathic interviewer who asks tough questions just to watch you suffer. If you receive a difficult question or two, this is usually because an interviewer is trying to learn a lot about you in a short period of time.

We know someone who interviewed for a position in business consulting who was asked how many windows there are on the island of Manhattan. That's certainly a difficult question, but it served a purpose. The interviewer wanted to determine whether or not this person was capable of thinking quickly and effectively on her feet.

Other sorts of difficult questions include matters that you would otherwise never discuss with a stranger (e.g., what is your biggest weakness?) or expert-level technical concerns (e.g., write a short program to forecast consumer behavior; sell me this pen). But again, interviewers don't ask these questions because they want you to fail.

Actually, the opposite is usually true. Interviewers have a job that they would like to fill. They have work that needs to be done. They are often busy and stressed. They are pretty sure you can do this job. Indeed, most interviewers want you to do well, because they want to make a hire and end their search. All you need to do is make them feel comfortable in their belief that you're a qualified candidate.

Myth: Some people are just bad at interviewing.

Truth: Well, actually, this one is a little bit true. Some people are mean, petty, or condescending, and aren't exactly a joy to work with. They tend to exhibit these traits in their interviews, which understandably don't go as well as they'd like. But because these people often don't recognize these traits in themselves, they also tend not to read books that are designed to help them become better at interviewing. This means that this probably doesn't describe you.

Most people who think that they're bad at interviewing are thinking about something else entirely. They think that because they're shy, socially anxious, or have noticeable reactions when they get nervous, they're always going to struggle with job interviews. But this only hurts people when they focus too much on the fact that they're blushing, stuttering, or appearing introverted, instead of focusing on the content of what they're saying. After all, people whom this describes are probably not interviewing for jobs that require perfect elocution or a flawless appearance. They're applying to jobs that are appropriate for their skills and that don't depend upon areas that are weaknesses for them. Good interviewers understand what their jobs require, and they don't get hung up on inconsequential details.

If you believed any of these myths, you're hardly alone. As our own early experiences made clear, we too misunderstood the point of the job interview. And we've seen many others—young and old, inexperienced and experienced—who lug these myths into interviews, usually to the detriment of their prospects. But now you know better: the purpose of the interview is to determine your alignment for a particular job, and interviewing well relies upon skills that you can improve.

SUMMARY

- Your goals and the interviewer's goals (evaluate whether you are a good match for the job) are aligned and not in opposition.
- Interview questions don't have "correct" answers; good answers depend upon individual personalities and individual situations.
- A successful interview might not result in a job offer, and that can be a good thing.
- *Anyone* can get better at interviewing.

CHAPTER 3: INSIDE THE MIND OF AN INTERVIEWER

We'll let you in on a little secret. Interviewers don't want to have to interview. They'd rather you were already hired. Of course, especially in growing organizations, they'll have to interview people frequently, but in their ideal situation, these future interviews would always be for new openings. What interviewers really don't want is to have to interview candidates for the position that's currently open. Ever again.

It's not that they hate interviewing, although it's certainly not everyone's favorite task. And it's not simply that interviewing regularly for the same position can be a drain on an organization's resources. Interviewers also don't want to be proven wrong. They don't want to be the person who recommended hiring someone whose performance turns out to be lackluster. They don't want to be the person who recommended hiring someone who later needs to be fired. They don't even want to be the person who recommended someone who quits after ten months.

Succeeding in job interviews involves understanding both sides of the conversation, your own and that of the people who want to fill the open position. If you can manage to think like your interviewers, you will be able to speak directly to their concerns and put yourself that much closer to landing a great job.

In order to understand what's going on in the minds of hiring managers and your potential bosses, it can be helpful to think about how the process often goes wrong. Here are a few profiles of people we've worked with over the years. To be clear, none of these profiles represents a single real person, but they're characteristic of many coworkers whom we've known. Each also indicates an interview process that could and should have gone differently.

The square peg. The square peg might have been great in the interview setting, but he can't actually do the job. To the interviewer, his previous experience seemed highly relevant, but it turned out to be insufficient for the present job. His coworkers might appreciate his water cooler banter, but his bosses must double-check or reassign most of his work. What's worse, the extra coaching and training that they provide don't seem to help. In worst-case scenarios, his employers have to fire him in order to protect their workflow, and this brings down office morale. Suddenly, people who didn't work closely with this misaligned employee are thinking, *Why are people being fired randomly? Is my job at risk? Maybe I should start looking for a more secure position myself.*

The slacker. Unlike the square peg, the slacker may be perfectly capable, but she doesn't seem to do much of anything. She can't be bothered to learn the details of a project before an important meeting with a client. She sometimes closes the door to her office and chats with her mother all day. (Office doors don't block out noise *that* well.) When she's in a meeting, she "secretly" plays games on her iPhone. (It is wholly obvious when you're checking your work email and when you're on Facebook.) To make matters worse, the slacker's inaction upsets her coworkers, whose jobs are now harder than they were before she was hired. They're silently aware that the slacker is being paid a salary to do nothing at all.

The troublemaker. The troublemaker is often capable, and he usually does the work that is asked of him. But he does something else that is certainly not asked of him. He creates unnecessary tension in the workplace. This may be done in the form of subtle (sometimes less-than-subtle) gossip: "Do you think Mark is gunning for a promotion? I heard he had coffee with the VP of finance yesterday." Or "I'm pretty sure this new so-called security protocol is actually a system to keep track of how much time we spend at our desks." This person complains about his coworkers, office policies, and employee pay, but always to other employees and never to someone who actually has the authority to answer his questions or remedy the problem. This person is rarely fired for failing to complete his work, but he's also less likely to be given a second chance if he makes a mistake. For most employers this is an even bigger disaster than it seems. The toxic culture created by this person makes his coworkers dissatisfied; indeed, sometimes these employees leave, giving the troublemaker a chance to begin again with new hires.

The achiever. The achiever is more than capable, highly engaged, even respectful of her bosses and coworkers. She's a dream employee except for one major issue: she wants more recognition, a better title, and better pay and she wants these things faster than the organization can accommodate. The achiever may do wonderful things and do them quickly, but she jumps ship and signs with a competitor as soon as she has new accomplishments to display. Suddenly, the organization's top competitor has a great employee, while they themselves are back to hiring.

The prima donna. Watch out. The prima donna may be a good, even a talented, employee but his performance is out of line with his self-perception. Like the achiever, he wants a raise and a promotion, but unlike the achiever, he has an unrealistic sense of the demand for his skills. He may not want to leave his job (indeed, he may be unable to do so), but he demands as much as he can while he waits for something better. A prima donna doesn't necessarily produce further rounds of hiring, but if your interviewer is an experienced hiring manager, they will do their best to avoid hiring this character. A prima donna creates tension. His manager is always saying no or bending over backwards to give him what he wants, like the best office or best projects. And if he gets what he wants and is paid more than his equally effective peers, his coworkers may become aware of that inequality and feel less satisfied with their own situations. He's also often the first person out the door when the economy goes sour, because cutting his salary from payroll is the best bang for the buck.

The job hopper. The job hopper also shares an important trait with the achiever. She's a competent worker, but she's not fully committed. She questions, *Am I meant to check tax returns or should I be in a forest in Canada, studying the migratory patterns of rare birds?* Or perhaps her boyfriend has a job offer across the country, and she wants to follow. The job hopper leaves as soon as it's convenient for her, regardless of how her schedule fits with her employer's needs.

These are caricatures, of course. Good interviewers don't try to force people into boxes. And there can be good reasons to act in each of these ways. Some are truly great reasons, like trying to achieve your real earning potential or supporting a loved one as they take up a new career. The important thing to keep in mind is that interviewers don't want to have to hire more often than needed for the same position. It's their task to determine not simply whether you have the right experience, an excellent degree, or a winning personality; they need to know that you'll serve the organization's larger interests.

WHAT TYPE OF EMPLOYEE ARE YOU?

To determine what kind of employee you are, a good interviewer will try to glean several pieces of information. Some of these pieces of information are really important. We call these *major considerations.* Nearly all interviewers think about all of the major considerations, and they think about them for nearly all job candidates. The other pieces of information that an interviewer wants to learn are *minor considerations.* Only certain interviewers care about the minor things, they may care about them only for certain jobs, and they may not think about them for all candidates.

All of these considerations are reliant on one thing: that you come across as being accurate during the interview. Interviewers need assurance that you are self-aware and that you are accurately describing your experience. If they think you're talented at saying what you think they want to hear, or that your self-perception is wildly different from the way others perceive you, they won't believe anything you have to say. Show yourself to be a reliable source of information by sharing examples that back up your claims.

MAJOR CONSIDERATIONS

From the standpoint of any organization, having to fire and then hire again is much worse than having to hire again because someone quit. Firing employees is unpleasant and costly, and it lowers morale. For this reason, the major considerations are competency, fit, and interest. If new employees don't meet the basic requirements for these considerations, they put their organizations at risk.

COMPETENCY

Basic competency is often the first quality that an interviewer tries to evaluate. It's good to remember that the evaluation of your competency begins before any representative of the organization shakes your hand or calls you on the phone. Before any interview, someone in the organization (usually multiple people) reviews your cover letter and resume. During this initial review, they ask themselves, "Can this applicant do the job?" And in order to answer this question, they'll look for relevant experience, knowledge, and the presence of particular skills.

If you're like many people (remember the obviously-strong-candidate approach?), you may be thinking that you spent hours and hours on your resume and it already explains your skills and abilities perfectly well, thank you very much. Why would an interviewer ask you about the same facts that you carefully listed for them already?

In a perfect universe, landing a job would be a simple matter of sending a resume. Alas, this is not the case. Resumes have a few key faults. As we mentioned earlier, they are short and can't come close to describing the full extent of your relevant experience, let alone your passion for the field. What's more, the language of resumes is highly, if sometimes intentionally, ambiguous: the same description of last summer's internship often masks wildly different levels of experience or proficiency. And finally—and it's unlikely that this refers to you—small numbers of people out and out lie on their resumes.

Interviewers are aware of these faults. And for this reason, they will usually ask questions about how long, how often, and at what level you have actually performed the tasks and duties that you described on your resume. How long did it take you to become a spreadsheet expert? Was that successful branding campaign on social media entirely your effort or did you make important contributions as part of a team? You don't need to have learned everything already, but you do need to be able to speak clearly and effectively about what you know and how you hope to develop in the future.

The final thing to keep in mind about the ambiguity of your resume is that interviewers often probe areas that seem like potential weaknesses. For instance, if the job posting mentions that effective employees will need to use Excel macros and you don't include anything about macros in your cover letter or resume, you will need to be prepared to answer a question about your ability or experience in this area. You needn't be an expert in macros, of course, to convey your general competence or your willingness to learn, but good preparation will lead you to expect this very question.

FIT

We've been throwing around the term "fit," but what does it actually mean? Fit is a catchall word to describe the fact that organizations want employees who can adapt easily to their roles, be successful, and contribute to the overall office culture. Fit is an elastic term. It means different things in different contexts.

Fit is sometimes a matter of the job in question. If a company is hiring a customer service representative, they may search for someone who is warm, supportive, and patient. These same qualities might ill serve someone who is a federal prosecutor. (No offense to federal prosecutors!) What's more, if an organization publicly espouses certain values, like its low environmental impact, a warm person who volunteers for local river clean-up days might be an even better fit.

Fit can also involve the changing needs of a particular department. If the interviewer thinks that the customer service department is doing exemplary work, he may refrain from hiring someone who comes across as highly assertive about her innovative vision for the future of the department. On the other hand, if the organization wants to overhaul its presently inefficient customer service program, this same assertive and innovative person might very well be a great fit. This is another reason not to blame yourself if you are not offered a particular job. You have no control over the specific (and often hidden) needs of individual organizations. Being a good fit means that people will understand you and accept you, that your competitive streak won't disrupt existing office harmony, or that your gift at consensus-building won't be suppressed by an autocratic boss. You won't be one of those troublemaking employees that hiring managers try to avoid.

Contrary to popular belief, fit is not whether the interviewer would enjoy having a working lunch with you or sitting next to you on a plane for a trip to visit a client. Rather, this is how some interviewers *intuit* fit. If they have a hard time figuring out whether your communication style or demeanor aligns with how work gets done at their organization, they sometimes chalk it up to personality or likeability and leave it at that.

Employers do sometimes use the word "fit" as a synonym for personality. Don't be tripped up by this. If an interviewer is looking for "the right personality," this usually doesn't mean that they are looking for someone with particularly high marks for extraversion or neuroticism on personality assessments. It more frequently means they want someone who will work well with their existing team. Interviews provide you with opportunities to show that you can do just this, whether by asking thoughtful questions, responding politely to introductions in the hallway, or demonstrating your familiarity with common tasks and procedures.

While you can't force fit and you shouldn't try to, you also shouldn't forget that an interviewer is looking for it. If you *are* a good fit, you should try to make this clear. To do so, don't just parrot an organization's website ("I value integrity, just like Acme, Inc. does"). Communicate your fit with examples (e.g., describing a time when you actually showed integrity).

INTEREST

The last of the major considerations is, in some sense, the hardest to understand. It is a genuinely surprising fact that many people go on interviews for jobs they don't actually want. They may be looking for practice. (We don't recommend this!) They may want to work for a particular organization and nurse a hope that by accepting an entry-level position that doesn't suit them, they will be positioned for a promotion some time later. Alternately, they may simply be in need of a paycheck and therefore willing to take any offer that comes their way.

No matter what the motivation, a fundamental lack of interest is off-putting to interviewers. Remember: interviewers work hard at their jobs, whether they manage the entire hiring process or help out by reading resumes and meeting with candidates. No one wants to invest precious time in the interview process and in drafting a job offer that has no chance of being accepted. (This goes doubly for people who simply want practice negotiating the terms of an offer.) Hiring managers also have no desire to hire someone who will continue to search for other jobs immediately after they enter their new position. Employees who have one foot out the door are less productive and often weigh heavily on office morale. For these reasons, employers rather reasonably want to know whether or not you are actually enthusiastic about the position and the larger organization.

MINOR CONSIDERATIONS

In addition to the major considerations of competency, fit, and interest, interviewers sometimes take into account less important considerations like your salary requirements or your future plans. For positions that have previously involved high turnover, for instance, interviewers may seek to understand how long you plan to stay in the position. Are you planning to move back to California within two years? Go to graduate school? Seek lightning fast career advancement? Start working part-time to spend more time at home with family? These issues aren't necessarily deal-breakers. Some positions are well-suited for people who don't plan to stay stationary for long. That's why these questions don't always arise in the mind of an interviewer.

Other less common considerations include:

- Whether the organization can afford you;
- How fast they might be able to train you;
- The potential fit between your work style and that of your would-be supervisor (i.e., a much more specific type of fit than your relationship to the larger organization);
- Whether you're able to meet the travel commitments necessary for the job;
- Whether you might be willing to move (if, for instance, they hope to place someone in a satellite office); and even
- Whether there are other, open positions in the company that would be a better match, even though you may be perfectly well qualified for the present one.

The task of the next several chapters is to show you how to communicate well and prepare for these considerations, both major and minor. When you find a job you're interested in, step away from your own priorities and think about those of your interviewer. Think about the fears that might come to their mind as they hire. Then, think about how you can assure the interviewer that you won't make their worst fears come true.

You may even use this process to help identify the best jobs to apply to in the future. If you think you might be an achiever, you might seek a job at an organization known for promoting from within, based on merit and not seniority. If you think you might be a job hopper, you could try a job that doesn't require months of training, so that your departure, whenever it is, doesn't burn bridges.

The interviewer's considerations will differ from one job to another, and from organization to organization. You won't be able to predict every consideration, but most are easy to enough to figure out. If you do this effectively, you are well on your way to being fully prepared.

SUMMARY

- Interviewers want to know whether you can actually do the job in question, and to determine this, they need more detail than what is on your resume.
- Interviewers want to know whether you will be a good fit for their organization and for the position itself.
- Interviewers want to know whether you actually want the job (not just any job).
- Interviewers need to develop confidence that what you say is accurate; otherwise, they may question your competency, fit, or interest.

CHAPTER 4: INTERVIEW STORYTELLING

It is not easy to give interviewers exactly what they want. They want to learn a lot about you in a short period of time. You may only have thirty minutes or an hour to convey all of your skills and knowledge, your enthusiasm, and your fit for the job. Initially, you may have even less time. (We know one professor who was asked to summarize her past, present, and future research agenda; teaching philosophy; and experience with departmental committees all in a single fifteen-minute screening interview. Yikes.) How can you communicate all of the information an interviewer wants to hear, clearly and concisely, but with enough detail and consistency that the interviewer believes they are getting an accurate sense of who you are?

The way we do this is to tell a story.

WHAT IS A STORY?

Jen walked into our studio for her mock interview in an enviable position. She had recently graduated from a great university and had a ton of work experience—even some that was directly related to the job she was hoping to get next: an administrative assistant position. Her friends expected that she would have no problem getting a job—quickly—and having a successful career.

To the untrained eye, her interview went well. She knew that she should seem enthusiastic and talk about the research she had done to learn about the organization she was "interviewing" with. (We asked people to show up with a specific job in mind; she was by far the best at convincing us that she was actually doing so during the interview.) She described her skills and experience clearly, had answers to all of the questions, and seemed like someone who would get along well with her coworkers.

But Charles, her interviewer, was confused. If he actually had a job opening like the one she wanted, he wasn't sure he would have bothered inviting Jen to interview for it. If he had interviewed her, he would definitely have doubts about hiring her. The problem? He couldn't understand why she wanted the job. She didn't fit his profile of the type of person who would apply for the position.

She wasn't overqualified in the sense some people mean it. She didn't hint that she would want a higher salary than the position would have commanded, she wasn't too experienced, and she didn't have the skills to be CEO instead.

Jen seemed odd for the job because she seemed to be a certain type of person, and that type of person tends to think of themselves as deserving a job with autonomy, responsibility, and decision-making authority. People who graduate from selective schools like her alma mater, the University of Michigan (UM), on-time and with good grades don't often aspire to be entry-level administrative assistants. We know this because we've met many recent UM graduates during our time in Ann Arbor, and until meeting Jen, neither of us had ever met one who aspired to a long career as an administrative assistant. The types of people who attend and graduate from UM usually expect to land "good" jobs, and are disappointed if they fall short of their expectations.

In Ann Arbor, entry-level assistant jobs are most commonly held by:

1. People who didn't graduate from UM (that is, graduates of other colleges, or people with little or no college education);

2. UM graduates who want to go to graduate school within two years (but need time off after finishing their undergraduate degree for a variety of reasons); or
3. UM graduates who can't get a job in the field in which they really want to work (because of a lack of work experience, mediocre grades, or other issues).

Of course, some of the people in the first and third categories also want to go to graduate school, but the fact that Jen had succeeded at UM placed her firmly in the second category in Charles' mind. His assumption about her was solidified because her undergraduate major—psychology—is a field that yields a lot of prospective graduate students.

So, Charles walked into the interview expecting Jen to say that she was looking for a job that capitalizes on the skills she's already developed, before going on to graduate school in a year or two. He wasn't trying to stereotype or pigeonhole her; like most interviewers, he was just trying to get a sense of what he should expect during the interview.

From childhood, humans categorize and use comparisons to learn. It's unrealistic to expect that an interviewer will meet you, having already decided that your resume was intriguing enough to spend time interviewing you, without having any preconceived notion of who you are. The interviewer may be a complete stranger to you, but you have already made an impression on the interviewer.

Jen started the interview by proudly saying she was from the south. If Charles had needed it, that was one final piece of information that screamed prospective graduate student. Most UM graduates who hail from other parts of the country don't stay in Ann Arbor after graduating. For those who do stay, it's usually because they haven't yet found a job that will relocate them or they don't want to bother moving so soon before moving elsewhere for graduate school. They rarely seem like they have a desire to permanently settle in Ann Arbor—it's just the place where they happen to be at the moment.

Charles was pretty confident he knew Jen's story for the first ten minutes of the interview. Then, as Jen described her college major, she casually said, "Quite honestly, none of the grad school programs really appeal to me."

Where was Charles left at this point? He didn't understand why she wanted this job. Was she lying about her aspirations for graduate school because she didn't want Charles to reject her in favor of someone who would stay in the job longer than a year? Was she trying to buy time in a starter-job while she figured out a graduate program that *did* appeal to her? Was she already convinced that she couldn't get a job that would be more aligned with her interests? She seemed genuinely interested in the job, but he couldn't figure out why.

This lack of understanding, the nagging feeling that Charles didn't know who she was, would have turned off most interviewers. It's not that interviewers are wedded to their initial impressions of job candidates. Revising their initial impressions is why they interview candidates instead of hiring them based on resumes alone. It's not a problem to say something that initially surprises an interviewer, as long as you help them understand why it all makes sense in the end. When an interviewer is left feeling confused about who you are at the end of an interview, they won't feel comfortable hiring you.

It took Charles a few minutes after the interview was over to think about what he had been hearing for the last half hour. Finally, the pieces clicked. He walked back into the studio to give her feedback and verify what she really wanted out of a job: flexibility. Most of the UM students we interviewed were looking for high-powered jobs that would demand many hours and be stressful, but also be financially and emotionally rewarding. Jen, on the other hand, wanted a job that wouldn't interfere with other aspects of her life, like family. And she specifically wanted to stay in Ann Arbor, the home of her long-term boyfriend. She had identified an administrative office role as one where she could put in normal hours, meet an employer's reasonable expectations, and still have time and energy for other things.

What Jen did during the mock interview was in line with most job search advice. What she could have done better was to think, ahead of time, about how her answers would fit together. What would a complete stranger understand about her, given her particular background, if she wasn't open about her ambitions? How could she tell someone about herself in a way that made sense? That's what we call a job interview story—the combination of your skills, knowledge, experience, interests, and other characteristics that paint a picture of you as a worker.

When we're talking about a story for an interview, we aren't talking about the kind of fiction you might read on the beach. An interview story is 100% non-fiction—a true-life story. It's not full of embellishments or fanciful details. A description of the time you won an award isn't aided by a weather report (*it was a dark and stormy night...*) and your telling of a time you worked on a team doesn't need any extra drama (*my teammate's friend turned out to have an evil twin; they'd been separated at birth...*). You don't need to evoke Tolkien, describing every detail in your journey. And your story isn't about making yourself sound more experienced than you are or assuming all the credit for group projects.

An interview story is simple: it's a summary of who you are as a worker. It includes your educational and work histories. It also includes your traits, skills, talents, work values, and interests. It's a coherent explanation of the decisions, choices, and events in your career pathway. Your story will show the interviewer why you applied for a particular job, how that job fits with your career plans, and what the interviewer can expect from you in the future.

Jen's story was that she was intelligent and a capable learner with work experience as an administrative assistant and in several related roles. She was a very adept organizer who enjoyed helping small business owners by taking care of the details for them. All of those pieces of her story came across clearly during her interview. For Jen, the missing piece was why she wanted to keep being an administrative assistant instead of using her degree to springboard to something more ambitious like most of her cohort. She didn't need to give lots of details—an interviewer doesn't need to know whether she was engaged or when she planned to get pregnant. But Jen did need to find a way to describe why an administrative assistant job fit with the career she wanted. The piece that was missing—that she had a reason to stay in the Ann Arbor area and wanted to prioritize work-life balance—would have made her story make sense. When she glossed over that vital information, her story neither fit with the common narrative for people like her nor did it add up to a sensible, if uncommon, narrative. An omitted motive made her entire story elusive.

WHY IS HAVING A STORY IMPORTANT?

The fact is, everyone has a story, whether they create it ahead of time or not. Interviewers naturally make assumptions about who you are based on your resume and cover letter, the way you act during the interview, and what you tell them. But your default story—the one an interviewer would walk away with if you didn't prepare ahead of time—may not be accurate and it may not be as compelling as it could be. If the story an interviewer hears doesn't help them understand your capabilities, your reasons for wanting the job, and your fit, you have lost an opportunity. If that story is confusing, vague, or inconsistent, you probably won't get a second chance to clarify who you really are. The best way to give the interviewer the right portrayal of yourself is to develop your story ahead of time and use it throughout your job search.

An interviewer's job is hard. Your preparation for the interview makes their job easier. When you're able to give a high-level summary of who you are as a worker and back it up with examples, they'll have an easier time figuring out what they need to know and remembering important pieces later on. When you can guess what they might assume about you that isn't true, you can quickly correct their perception and get them on track to understanding your unique story.

Creating a story takes more time than the normal version of interview preparation. But good interview preparation *should* take time. After all, good jobs are hard to find and are worth the effort. By putting in effort to prepare for interviews, you won't have to go through as many interviews to land a great job. Furthermore, the benefits of creating a story start early and will last throughout your entire job search.

Children are asked what they want to be when they grow up from a very young age. If you're like most people, your first answers involved jobs you saw around you or in your favorite books. Perhaps you wanted to be a teacher, a doctor, or an astronaut. As you grew up and learned about different subjects in school, your list of career options simultaneously widened and became more specific. They widened because you learned about jobs you didn't know about as a young child, and they became more specific because you started to learn about what you were good at and what you liked doing. You might think of this process as proto-story development.

For most people, this process continues throughout high school and into college. Young adults keep learning about different possible jobs, and as they do, they think about whether they have—or can acquire—the skills needed to do those jobs well. They think about whether they like the general work environments associated with particular jobs, like being active and on their feet, sitting at a desk all day, traveling frequently, and so forth. They think about whether these daily activities are interesting, and whether these career paths seem rewarding. Whether this process is done consciously and deliberately or somehow just happens, this process essentially involves using your story, as it develops, to narrow your career goals and begin preparing for your job search.

Clarity about your own story can also help you decide which specific job ads to apply to and which jobs to skip over. Think back on your past experiences within organizations, whether those experiences were paid work, internships, volunteering, being part of a student or community group, or even just working with a small team for a class project. What did you like and not like about those experiences? Reflections on the past should help you decide what you are looking for in a new organization.

When Kevin was hired, he had been told that his position was newly created, the first of many in response to an organizational decision to double in size within five years. He was excited to be part of a dynamic company, in a job that seemed tailor-made for the skills he learned in his classes. But as the company grew, targets started to shift. Priorities for new projects started to conflict with priorities for legacy projects, and suddenly there wasn't much support for the specific work that he was doing. Kevin sought clarification about what he should do and how, and he got different answers from different people. After a year of this, Kevin vowed that he would never work at a rapidly growing company again.

You can do your own reflections by carefully reading a job description, browsing the organization's website, and thinking about whether it sounds like the type of place you wouldn't mind spending your time. If you loved the intensity of the hack-a-thon you participated in, you might seek out organizations that describe a "fast-paced work environment." On the other hand, if a summer job as a customer service representative left your head spinning by the end of the day from non-stop phone calls, you might want to avoid organizations that describe themselves as fast-paced. If you felt like you had no room to grow at your last company, you might want to focus on larger organizations or ones that are known for promoting from within. If your last job was at an organization that kept laying people off, you may find that it's preferable to look only at jobs in really stable or growing industries. None of this negates the need to keep evaluating the organization and its employees during your interview, but you might as well start early and target your efforts to applying to jobs at organizations in which you're more likely to fit. In the long run, doing this will save you time.

YOUR STORY WRITES YOUR COVER LETTER

Better yet, even after you've learned to target your job applications to the types of organizations and jobs where you will indeed thrive, your story continues to be valuable. While you're preparing your application materials, your story helps you to describe how your experience and unique skills match up with the job requirements. If your story is straightforward, you can write your cover letter in a way that confirms that your background is just what an interviewer might expect. Or perhaps your cover letter might explain a more complicated story, like motivations for switching industries or the reason for a gap in work history.

When Emily was applying for jobs after a postdoctoral position in North Carolina, she was determined to turn her long-distance relationship back into a regular one by returning to Michigan. She knew that the organizations she was applying to might be wary of interviewing someone who was out of state, even someone who was qualified and had a history in the region. So at the end of her cover letter, she wrote: *I am moving back to Ann Arbor in August and will be visiting on weekends until then. I can easily extend one of these trips to accommodate an interview.* With this addition, she indicated why she was bothering to apply to far-away jobs (i.e., they wouldn't be far-away for long) and that the organization wouldn't have to jump through hoops or pay for a flight and hotel just to interview her.

YOUR STORY HELPS YOU PRACTICE EFFICIENTLY

While you're preparing for the interview, you can also use your story to practice answering questions. You'll rarely be able to guess every question that will be asked during an interview. Using your story as a guide will make it easier to be prepared for surprises. Learn how to incorporate the important elements of your story into your answers, and it will start to come naturally. Even if you've never thought about the answer to a particular question, you'll know what you want to say, and you'll have examples in mind to draw from. (We go over this in greater detail in Chapters Ten and Eleven.)

YOUR STORY PREVENTS CONFUSION

Knowing your story not only helps you to think about what to say during an interview, it also helps you to suppress things you *shouldn't* say.

During our mock interviews, we rarely asked questions that couldn't be anticipated ahead of time. Yet we noticed that, time and time again, job seekers gave confusing answers. Sometimes these answers were confusing because they seemed contradictory or vague. Other times, they simply didn't give us the clarity and peace of mind of knowing that this job seeker was who we expected them to be—someone who could be a great new hire.

Mock interviewee Sean was one of these candidates. He was practicing for internship interviews; his ideal summer position would be focused on public policy and located in Washington DC. He had clearly thought about his answers to many of our questions, and he knew how to present a professional image. Charles asked him a straightforward question about how he ended up at UM. Sean replied:

> I was born in Midland, Michigan. After the sixth grade, my father took a new job on the East Coast. So we moved out to the Philadelphia area. But I always stayed close to my roots of Michigan. I think it made me more proud to be a Michigander, being in a different state; it was definitely a very different environment in Pennsylvania. I kind of grew up and matured a Michigan fan, so when it came time to apply to colleges, Michigan was one of my top two choices.

As a stand-alone answer to a question about why he attended UM, this was a reasonable answer. But as he explained why he wanted to return to Michigan, Sean also declared himself an outsider to the East Coast. His identity seemed contradictory with his desire for a policy career in DC.

Interviewers know that when people dislike the place where they live, they become dissatisfied, both with their jobs (if that's what is keeping them in that horrible place) and with life in general. An interviewer in DC might hear Sean's answer and wonder whether he would get homesick or be willing to compromise about where he lives in order to have the career he desires. No interviewer is going to want to make you miserable just because you're willing to take a job.

We're pretty sure Sean didn't mean to communicate that location was extremely important to him. If Sean had instead focused on communicating his story—and only his story—he would have known which details of this answer were extraneous. He could have focused on the fact that he knew Michigan was a good school, which would have been a true answer and one that wasn't at odds with the rest of his story, namely an interest in working for an organization in DC. The apparent contradiction between his identity and his career goals was really the difference between who he used to be (a Michigander) and who he is now (someone who is passionate about public policy and who perhaps has learned a thing or two about adjusting to a move). By thinking about your story ahead of time, you can identify facts about yourself that are too complex to communicate in a short thirty-minute or even an hour-long interview. Those facts might explain who you are—they are part of your life story, after all—but they don't need to be included in your interview story.

YOUR STORY SHOWS ACCURACY

Finally, to convince an interviewer that *they* know who you are, you must first convince them that *you* know who you are. And the best way to do that is to have a really solid understanding of who you are. Of course you know yourself well. But interviewers want to know that you are aware of how you compare to other people, and that you have an idea of who you will be in the future.

Knowing your story and being able to tell it can be the difference between a frustrating, uncommunicative interview and one that puts your best self forward. Imagine for a moment that you're a Business Finance Officer with TIAA-CREF in Manhattan, and you're hoping to hire a new financial analyst. You interview two candidates, Chris and Sam, on consecutive days:

> You: Where do you want to be in five years?
>
> Chris: Well, I think that I'm really going to like being a financial analyst and that I'll want to keep doing that. I also might go to graduate school in a few years.
>
> You: Why should I hire you instead of someone else?
>
> Chris: I'm a really hard worker, and I really want this job.

Chris's answers seem rather vague, don't they? There was a hint of interest, some suggestions of positive traits, but nothing that seemed really convincing. Chris doesn't seem to know her story and certainly doesn't know how to communicate that story to others.

In comparison, Sam gives very different answers:

> You: Where do you want to be in five years?
>
> Sam: My internship taught me that I will really enjoy being a financial analyst. Five years from now, I expect that I will have earned a senior analyst title. Also, I expect I'll need to be staying on top of developments in the field, so I may start a Master's program part-time after work.
>
> You: Why should I hire you instead of someone else?
>
> Sam: Compared to the other interns I worked with last summer, I seemed to have more financial acumen and understanding of the technical requirements of the job. I could tell that my hard work in classes really paid off in that respect.

If you knew nothing but what they wrote on their resumes and said in their interviews, would you have more confidence hiring Chris or Sam? Chris and Sam could have had exactly the same stories on paper: they could have attended the same college, earned the same grades, and even had the same internship. But Sam has thought through his story and can easily share examples and evidence that back up his claims. He knows himself, and it shows.

SUMMARY

- Interviewers will have assumptions about you, which may or may not be true, before the interview begins.
- The best way to approach an interview is to tell your story, which is your summary of who you are as a worker. Your story is the combination of your educational and work histories, your

traits, skills, talents, work values, interests, decisions, and motives. It is a cohesive narrative that explains the trajectory of your career from the past through your future plans.

- Your story can help you as you look for jobs, because knowing where you came from can help you understand where you should go and who you'll be in the future.
- Using your story as a framework helps you to identify and deliver examples that make sense to interviewers.

CHAPTER 5: YOUR DEFAULT STORY

In the last chapter we introduced you to Jen, a recent graduate who was looking for a job as an administrative assistant. She didn't realize it, but interviewers were making assumptions about her. Interviewers will make assumptions about you too. Sometimes, their pre-conceived notions might be spot on. Other times, they will be near the truth, but not entirely accurate. And you may encounter situations in which interviewers believe things to be true about you that are absolutely inaccurate.

Just like Jen, the best way to deal with these inaccurate perceptions is to tell your story clearly. Something that makes this easier is to have a sense of what others might be thinking about you. After all, if someone already believes something about you that is true, all you need to do is confirm it. If someone believes the opposite of what's true about you, you'll have to break them of their erroneous belief as well as convince them of what is really true. If you can guess ahead of time which aspects of your story an interviewer will have trouble understanding, you'll know where to focus your efforts so that you're understood.

HOW DO YOU APPEAR?: AN ACTIVITY

We have designed an activity to help you gain some perspective about what others might assume about you. To do this activity, the only thing you'll need is a piece of paper (and a pen, pencil, marker, even a crayon) or a blank document on your computer. (Keep in mind that it's not really the same to just think about all of this in your head. No one does things as thoroughly and diligently in their head as they do when they're writing by hand or typing. Plus, it will be handy to have a written record of this exercise that you can revisit to prepare for subsequent interviews.) Your resume could come in handy too, if you can't remember what's on it.

We'll begin by outlining what we call your default story. This is the story that interviewers might tell themselves *before* meeting you. It's the version with which you'll need to align your true story, or to which you'll juxtapose your true story, depending upon how different these stories are. As you think through the questions below, make sure to include both positive and negative things. (Some will be neutral.) Above all, think broadly.

You'll be thinking about yourself from the outside. You know things about yourself that others don't. For now, don't get caught up in those details. The point of this exercise is to paint a broad picture of yourself, as others see you. For that reason, our advice is to not think of yourself as you answer the following questions. Instead, think of someone who is like you in just the same area in which the question is focused. Don't try to be right or politically correct. Think about your gut instincts, and what others' instincts are likely to be.

As you work through the answers to the questions below, take the time to jot down your answers.

EDUCATION

What do people typically think about students who attend your college? What reputation do they have? (Is it a party school, where most students seem to enjoy socializing and having fun? Is it a more studious school, where most students know how to focus for long periods of time? Is it a commuter college that draws mostly local students who can't or don't want to leave the area?)

Do people with your credentials often go on to receive more education (e.g., finish an uncompleted degree or go to graduate school)? If so, when?

What types of students are drawn to your major? How do those students think and act differently than students with other majors? What skills do they have? What skills might they be perceived to lack?

What kinds of post-college career tracks do most people in your major pursue?

WORK

What types of people are attracted to the career field that you've chosen (or within which you have applied to jobs, if you're still a little up in the air)?

Who has the type of work experience that you already have? What types of careers do those people go on to occupy?

Is there a socioeconomic background that seems common among people with your past employment pattern (e.g., working only during the summer versus working while taking classes)?

What would you think about someone who, on paper at least, had the same number of jobs or internships for the same amount of time as you?

What might people in the interviewer's *location* think about people who live in your current location? (You might, for instance, think about regions of the country, about specific cities and their reputations, or about the differences between urban and rural communities.)

What are some common perceptions of people who grew up where you did (if that place is different from where you live now)?

What are some stereotypes about people your age or people of your generation? How are they perceived to work? What are their expectations? What are their most common career plans? (Remember, we aren't asking you to think about the truth here—just stereotypes.)

What are some stereotypes about people who look like you? These should include ideas that are based on your perceived race, ethnicity, and gender, but also other physical characteristics like your weight, height, attractiveness, and a host of other things. Even hairstyles say something—will you get a manicured haircut or style before your interview, or will you wear your hair loosely?

Who tends to participate in the activities in which you participate? What might someone assume about your values or interests based upon your extracurricular activities? (Think, in particular, about the titles of those activities. Phi Beta Kappa (an honors society) sounds a lot like Gamma Phi Beta (a social sorority) or Epsilon Sigma Alpha (a co-ed community service fraternity). An interviewer might have the wrong impression about you unless you're clear about the types of organizations to which you belong or what you do within those organizations.)

NOW ... STEP BACK

You don't have to limit yourself to these questions; you should use them instead to spark thoughts about your life as it might be perceived from the outside. Take the time now to think about any other things that are relevant to your circumstances. Pay special attention to anything that appears in your resume and cover letter.

Finally, think about the picture that gets created when you piece together each of the specific aspects that you thought about. This picture is your default story. You can use the space below, or use whatever style makes sense to you. (You might compose a short profile in prose, make a word cloud, or construct a list of important phrases.) Remember, the goal of this exercise is to learn to see yourself in broad strokes.

These are things people might think about me before they talk to me:

- _____

- _____

- _____

- _____

- _____

- _____

- _____

- _____

- _____

- _____

- _____

AN EXAMPLE

Let's use Emily as a guinea pig. Here are a few of the things that people might think about her, based solely upon her resume:

> Emily earned a BA from Penn State. Since Penn State is a popular state school, odds are she grew up in Pennsylvania. Penn State's admissions standards (average GPA and SAT scores) are selective but not highly selective, so she probably did pretty well academically in high school, but not well enough to go to a more prestigious college.
>
> Emily got her PhD from the University of Michigan five years later. That means that she did well academically in college and probably went straight to graduate school from her undergraduate degree. (It's uncommon to receive a PhD in less than five years in the United States.) She studied education and psychology, so she probably wanted a career in academia. Since a PhD is a terminal degree, she's unlikely to ever go back to school.
>
> After completing a postdoc, Emily seems to have switched fields entirely: her next job was in healthcare research. That's unusual, so maybe it means she failed to get a professorship or perhaps she was burned out by her graduate studies. She worked at one organization for seven years—so she's probably not at risk of job-hopping—and then she co-founded a company. Maybe that shift to self-employment was an attempt to balance work with raising kids? Based on the dates on her resume, she's perfectly within the age range during which highly educated mothers often have young children. (The median age of first birth among women with at least a master's degree is currently 30 years old.)

Some of these statements are true and some are not. Some, Emily thinks of as positive, while others not so much. Keep in mind that, for the purposes of this exercise, none of *her* judgments matter; all that matters is the way that others may perceive her (or you). Emily's default story would be different if she went to a private college in Texas instead of the state university in her hometown. An interviewer would have different thoughts about her if she was currently working in Los Angeles or if she was working in a small town in Idaho.

If you find yourself disagreeing with any of the concepts or statements you used to describe how people might perceive you, you now understand the importance of being able to tell *your* story. If you imagine most interviewers greet you without having made any assumptions or judgments about you and your background, you're wrong. Everybody walks into the interview setting and faces beliefs like these, and your story is your way to communicate what's true and what isn't.

SUMMARY

- Interviewers will make common assumptions about you based upon your resume and cover letter as well as their own beliefs.
- Identifying potential misconceptions will help you to correct them during the interview.

If Eric were a character in a movie, his life story would be pretty familiar. He went to college without clear ideas about his future career. His interests led him to take classes in many different fields; he switched majors several times and eventually chose history because, when he had to decide, it happened to be the major in which he had the most credits. With graduation looming and no obvious career path, he decided to follow the advice he had been given to "do what you love." For Eric, this meant traveling.

He jumped in head first, teaching English in a remote village in Southeast Asia. He was a fish out of water, but he loved it. After that job ended, he backpacked for several months, meeting other young people in hostels and getting to know the cultures of various countries he'd only dreamed about visiting before. Only once did he really fear for his life, when he caught a ride from a stranger on the back of a motorcycle. (Drivers' skill levels vary in every country, apparently!)

From there, he returned to the United States, but he didn't stay put. He jumped from city to city, and then traveled through South America, picking up whatever odd jobs he could find.

Eric had truly found something he enjoyed doing with his life, but being a member of the gig economy is a hard way to pay the bills. He decided to settle down a little—not to quit traveling entirely, but to start the path toward a career. Law seemed to be a good fit. Eric was accepted into law school without much difficulty, and he did well in his classes. Classes in international human rights were his clear favorites, and they solidified his interest in that area of law. Finally, he landed a clerkship in his chosen niche—in The Hague, no less (more travel!). As a clerk in The Hague, he had the opportunity to summarize evidence against a warlord who had been accused of recruiting child soldiers.

This, at any rate, is the story we heard during his mock interview. It makes a good deal of sense. It's easy to imagine the person Eric was as a college student and then in the short years that followed. If you enjoy traveling, it's easy to empathize with his interests, even to visualize many of his great adventures. You can probably also understand his decision, after years of cobbling together a fun, but necessarily frugal life, to seek more financial security.

Eric's story was a great place to begin an interview story, but it was only that—a beginning. Eric clearly had the skills and knowledge to succeed as a lawyer. But what about his interest in the actual job and his fit in an organization where people care strongly about human rights? Those were questionable.

To many interviewers, Eric's description of his past interests, motivations, and experiences might convey the impression that he had stumbled onto a legal career for no particular reason. Interviewers know that you won't stay in a job you hate, and that means that they want to understand what will *keep* you in a job for a long time. What duties and responsibilities might Eric be looking for at work? What kind of work environment would he enjoy? Would he be as engaged as his colleagues?

For his interview, Eric's story should have been much more strongly focused on communicating why he had chosen international human rights law rather than another law specialty. Not everyone has a good reason for this kind of choice, but Eric did and it needed to be front and center. As it happened, Charles found out about it almost by accident; after hearing the story above in its entirety, he had a hunch that something was missing. Charles doesn't normally ask this type of question, but he tried it out anyway: "Is there anything that you saw or experienced that pushed you in the direction of international law?"

This was Eric's reply:

> There actually is one specific memory I have as far as getting me on a route where I wanted to engage with social justice issues and international law specifically. When I went to South America, we flew into Rio de Janeiro; we were in Rio for a whole week. I got to see the *favelas*, the slums there. I met this Brazilian guy who took me on tour. Seeing how 100,000 people can live in that compact of a space, with I think four or five streets, and thousands and thousands of alleyways. Seeing how drug gangs ran the whole place, and poverty on that scale. It was an important afternoon for me. It really got me on the track that I ended up going: human rights work, development work, social justice issues. That's what I want to do now.

That was what Charles had been wanting to hear. Eric should have been itching to share this anecdote from the moment he entered the room, rather than waiting until the rest had been said.

To help an interviewer feel comfortable hiring him, Eric's story should be revised. That doesn't mean he needs to lie or hide things about himself. It just means that Eric needs to place emphasis on facts that will help an interviewer understand the most important parts of who he is.

These are the most important pieces of Eric's interview story:

- He went to college not really knowing what he wanted to do as a career, but he knew that he wanted to travel and understand the ways people live in other parts of the world.
- After graduating, Eric traveled as much as he could. During his travels, he saw the face of poverty and crime, and gained a strong desire to do whatever he could to fix these problems.
- Human rights, international development, and social justice are the issues about which he feels most passionate.

- Eric wants to use his knowledge of law and the empathy he has for people living in poverty and violence to help people around the world.
- He also has relevant experience with international treaty law and in writing memos and briefs from his clerkship in The Hague.

Eric's interview story might also include the following facts, when it's possible to share them:

- His travels weren't vacations; they were learning experiences. Eric had fun, but he also made a difference in people's lives, teaching English in Thailand and Argentina and teaching disadvantaged children in America.
- Eric doesn't have to rely on a theoretical understanding of how cultures differ: he's seen these differences firsthand.
- His background as a history major taught him how sociopolitical structures and historical movements can shape cultures decades or even centuries later, as well as why there are cultural differences in what are understood as human rights.
- His recent studies in law taught him what he needs to know to contribute to an organization that is dedicated to advancing international justice.

The rest of Eric's life story might make an appearance if he's asked about it, but those details shouldn't take up much time during an interview until he's finished communicating these more important facts.

WHAT MAKES A STORY?

When most people think about stories, they call to mind the traditional narratives that they read in books. We are *not* trying to teach you to tell this kind of story. We're talking instead about a type of story that is specific to the interview process. The story that you communicate during your interview needs to be focused on what you'll bring to your next job. When we say your story is about who you are as a worker, we mean that it's a story about your skills and knowledge; your interest in a specific job; your broader career plans; and your fit in a specific organization. All of these qualities depend upon your values, preferences, and behaviors. In other words, your story is based on your life, but it is not your life story.

If you're wondering at this point, "What is *my* story?" you're not alone. You know an enormous number of facts and anecdotes about yourself. But unfortunately, the sheer vastness of this information can make the task of winnowing this information into a single, comprehensible story an overwhelming challenge. Which details need to be communicated during an interview, and which details muddle the essence? Novels with complex characters are often called doorstoppers for a reason: it's hard to explain an interesting person and what happens to them in less than 500 pages. You don't have that luxury; in all likelihood, you have less than an hour to tell your story to an interviewer.

Luckily, you don't need a richly detailed and unique narrative; all you need is a set of facts that makes sense, is backed up by examples, and can be understood by someone who is trying to get a sense of your near-term future. And yet, it's not quite as easy as it sounds. If you think about the facts of your life that relate to your career development, they're probably very easy to understand when they're told in order. That story has a beginning (probably sometime in high school, maybe earlier or later), a middle (your educational and work-related training and experiences thus far) and an end (your exceptional capabilities, interest, and fit for this particular job). But during an interview, your story will *not be told that way*. It will be told in very short segments. And in all likelihood, you won't be able to choose the order of those segments. (You can guess some of the types of questions that you will be asked, but you won't know in what order they will be asked.)

And that, fundamentally, is why it's really, really important to think about your story ahead of time. What are the very most important aspects of your story, the ones that you *must* convey? What are the other components that you should try your darnedest to communicate? What is just filler that might be told in the linear version of your story, but which doesn't have to make its way into an interview?

We like to think of building a story as being like building a house. First, you need a foundation. That foundation is the underpinning of the other components of your story: all of the subsequent details rest on this base. In your story, the foundation is the sum of your life experiences. It's who you've known and how these people have influenced you. It's composed of core motivations and values that are consistent over time, even if what holds your interest changes from year to year. It's who you are—your identity. It's how you've gotten to where you are today.

On top of a building's foundation rests its frame. The walls of a home go a long way toward creating the character of a home. How many rooms are there, and how large are they? Is it a ranch house, two-story, something larger? In your story, the frame is who you are *today*: this includes your knowledge, skills, current interests, and your fit with a particular organization. These characteristics have their basis in your past experiences, just as a building's frame lies upon its foundation.

No building lasts for long without one final component—a roof. A roof holds the frame together and fulfills one of the basic functions of any home—keeping rain and snow off our heads. Until the roof is there, no one wants to live in a house. The roof of your story is made of the examples that you give in order to prove that the rest of your story is true.

Each of the components of this building is structural; they work together. A building without a foundation collapses as the ground shifts over time; a building without a frame (like a lean-to) doesn't make a very appealing house; and a building without a roof isn't a trustworthy way to protect yourself from the elements. Houses don't function well until all three components are in place.

Likewise, a story without a foundation may come across as incoherent; it may feel like you don't stand on solid ground. And if an interviewer doesn't hear about your skills, interests, and fit—your frame—they won't have a reason to want to hire you. And finally, if you don't provide your interviewer with examples, your claims about who you are may seem shaky and disjointed. A well-built story connects these three components to provide a strong, coherent, and compelling story that is backed up by evidence.

In Eric's case, his foundation is his love of travel, his interest in learning about new cultures, and his academic prowess. These are the things that led him to find his true career interests, and they will probably continue to be true for a long time. His frame consists of all of the skills and knowledge that he learned in law school, his interest in and passion for international human rights, and his ability to fit with an organization that is committed to international social justice. And Eric's roof is made up of interesting examples, like the very important experience he had in Rio de Janeiro, the details of his time as a clerk in The Hague, and his teaching experience. Taken together, these elements create a story that is both understandable and persuasive.

SUMMARY

- To effectively communicate who you will be in a new job, you need to identify the elements of your working life that are the most important to convey and focus on communicating these elements in your interview.
- Your story is based on your life, but it is not your life story.
- You probably won't be able to tell your story in a linear fashion, so your story needs to be coherent and consistent.
- You can think of your story as consisting of a foundation, a frame, and a roof, just like a house.

CHAPTER 7: STARTING TO BUILD YOUR STORY

The only person who can build your story is you, but we can help. We're about to ask you to do a bunch of exercises. Take your time with them. Doing these exercises well will set you apart from other job seekers who practice by merely answering a few example questions.

The exercises in this chapter are designed to be broad. In the next chapter, you'll have the opportunity to do exercises that will help you to prepare for an interview for a particular job. Taken in combination, these two sets of exercises are designed to go from broad outlines about your story to specific details for a reason: in order to tell your story effectively, you will need to modify it slightly for different jobs. That's not because you're pretending to be someone you're not. We start in broad outline because you have a complex story to tell, and in order to get at all of the rich content in your life that *might* work its way into your interviews, you'll need to consider the whole you. And we move to specific details because you'll have just a small amount of time with an interviewer during which you'll need to help them understand who you will be in that particular job.

How people act depends upon context. People act differently in very formal workplaces than they do in really casual ones. Now, you might prefer one of those environments to the other; in fact, your preference might be so strong that you don't apply to certain organizations. But people naturally act differently in different organizations, while at the same time remaining true to who they are.

This means that it's perfectly reasonable to use different sets of examples—all based on who you are as a whole person—for different jobs. Because each set of examples is grounded by the same foundation, we'll start by working on your foundation. You can think of everything in this chapter as groundwork that could be laid before your next job interview is scheduled. In the next chapter, you'll have the chance to prepare for a specific interview.

THE FOUNDATION

First we need to dig deep. Some stories are easy to tell, and some—like Jen's—are harder; they require more nuance. Regardless of their complexity, however, *all* stories become easier to understand with a little preparation.

THINK ABOUT YOUR WHYS

The whys we're referring to here are your past and present motivations. Why did you go to the college you went to? Why did you choose your field of study? Why did you (or didn't you) join that student group, study abroad, work a part-time job, or take extra courses over the summer?

Pay attention both to your *interests*, or the things that you like learning about and that hold your attention longest, and your *values*, or the qualities you regard highly and that you might want in a job. Common work-related values include: prestige, job security, financial reward, integrity, being useful, and the chance to learn, to be creative, or to help others. (There are many more.) What values do you hold that influence the decisions you make, or the way you make those decisions? What core interests have you held for a long time, even if the way you have experienced these interests has changed?

Interviewers will be listening for your whys. They'll interpret your past decisions and motivations in order to predict your future decisions, behaviors, and success in their organization. For instance, if you joined a lot of student groups because you love meeting and interacting with new people, you might look for a job that gives you opportunities to do just that. Being able to convey this motivation to an interviewer will help them understand the kind of job you're looking for and how you might fit with the role they are hoping to fill.

Below, we've listed a few examples of overarching motives that people bring to their professional lives. Go ahead and circle any of these that seem to *best* explain why you tend to do things or make certain choices. Add any more motivations that come to mind.

- Competition (i.e., doing better than someone else)
- Wanting security, financial or otherwise
- Avoiding something you're afraid of
- Becoming famous
- Being able to care for a loved one
- Having a sense of belonging in a group or community
- Being able to express yourself or be true to yourself
- Having the chance to learn new things
- Creating something that will outlast you

- _____

- _____

- _____

- _____

THINK ABOUT YOUR TURNING POINTS

Turning points are those times in your life in which you changed fundamental direction. Eric's tour of Rio de Janeiro's *favelas* was a turning point in his life: before that, he had lacked career direction, and then he found it. Perhaps you had planned to pursue one career, but had a moment when you realized that career wasn't right for you. For Emily, one turning point was a series of conversations during her year as a postdoctoral researcher; these conversations made her realize that she was more interested in doing research than the other tasks that are required for a successful career in academia (e.g., teaching, applying for grants, doing committee work). She turned away from the goal of becoming a professor and turned toward a job where she had the chance to play with giant data sets. Perhaps you made a new group of friends, moved to a new town, or had another kind of experience that made you see things in a different light. Any moment when you stopped going down one path and started going down another path constitutes a turning point. Make a list of your turning points below.

My turning points:

- _____

- _____

- _____

- _____

Take a minute to reflect. How did these experiences change you? Why did they change you? Understanding who and what has had an influence on the path your life has taken can help you gain perspective on what types of experiences you may want to seek out (or avoid) in the future. You should keep these experiences in mind as you evaluate the organization and your potential boss during the interview in order to make sure that the job is the right fit. Understanding your turning points can also help you to recognize how you react in stressful situations, how you respond to change, and what might help you stay on your chosen career path in the future.

In addition to turning points, you've probably had moments of which you are very proud and others of which you are less than proud. What did you learn about yourself from these experiences? Did they reinforce your decision to pursue a certain career path? Did they confirm that a particular field of study wasn't right for you? Did you learn what you are "made of"?

These stand-out experiences may not appear on your resume, but they make up the heart of your story's foundation. What moments do you hope you can avoid forevermore? And what will you need to do to make sure these moments don't happen again? How did you reach your pinnacle moments? What moments do you want to replicate as much as possible, and how can you put yourself in a position to do so in the future? Put these moments on paper by completing the following sentences:

- I hope to never again experience…

    _____.

- I'm going to try to avoid…

    _____.

- I got into those negative experiences because…

    _____.

- To escape future negative experiences, I should…

    _____.

- The best experience(s) I've ever had was/were…

    _____.

- I was most proud of myself when…

_____.

- I was able to have those great experiences because…

_____.

- I'm going to have more great experiences by…

_____.

Thinking about these things not only speaks to your goals for the future, but also to how you have improved from the past. Interviewers will listen to how you have responded to adversity. Good interviewers won't be put off by mistakes or failures in your past, as long as you've learned from these mistakes and have better strategies for the future. Likewise, they want to know that your achievements weren't merely flukes; they want to be reassured that you know how to continue your successes in the future.

THINK ABOUT WHAT PEOPLE TEND TO SAY ABOUT YOU

What are the common ways that people describe you? Don't just think about your friends; how have past teachers, bosses, coworkers, or others described you? Do these descriptions have anything in common? What makes you similar to other people who are looking for the same types of jobs? What makes you unique?

Pause. If you've read through these exercises so far and haven't found yourself setting the book aside and doing some thinking and writing, do it now. We'll still be here when you're done.

Now, if your parents are available, call them. Ask:

> What did my elementary school teachers say about me during parent-teacher conferences? What did they write on my report cards?
>
> What did your friends say about me?
>
> What did my friends' parents say about me?
>
> What are some things you've always known to be true about me?

While you have them on the line, you might as well ask about anything else that isn't clear to you yet. Try questions like:

> How do you think I've changed since I was a kid? How have I changed since just a few years ago?
>
> What qualities (skills/abilities/traits/knowledge) do you think I have now that will serve me well in my career? In life?
>
> What qualities (skills/abilities/traits/knowledge) do you think I could probably still work on? If I could learn or develop one thing that would make me even more successful in ten years, what would it be?

If you can't call your parents, ask your siblings, other family members, or long-term friends these questions. Once you're done, summarize what they told you and what you've heard from other people over the years.

These are things people think are true of me:

- _____

- _____

- _____

- _____

The opinions that other people have about you may not have anything to do with your career, but it's good to keep them in mind as you develop your story.

THINK ABOUT WHAT PEOPLE *DON'T* SAY ABOUT YOU

It's not just what people say about you that you should be paying attention to. What are some ways you've heard other people described, but that never get said about you? These can be either positive or negative. You may be the "funny, free-spirited one" in your family, and your sister might be the "hardworking one." Have classmates said things like, "I'm impressed you finished that project" but not "I'm impressed you put so much effort into that project"? Have managers ever said, "I admire how well you get along with customers" but never "I admire your work ethic"? Taken together, these types of comparisons don't mean you can't work hard, but they do suggest that your work ethic may be relatively average, rather than remarkably strong. A job candidate who isn't known for working very hard may not want to choose that quality as part of the foundation of their story.

These are things people *don't* seem to think are true of me:

- _____

- _____

- _____

- _____

THINK ABOUT YOUR SKILLS, KNOWLEDGE, AND ABILITIES

You are a complex person with many strengths. Some of these strengths are most obvious in a work setting (like your knowledge of legal precedent), others are obvious all the time (like your physical strength and ability to lift heavy objects), and some are mostly apparent outside of work (like your ability to train your pet). In this next exercise, we want you to figure out which of your qualities are most important to the foundation of your interview story.

The activity involves working with a worksheet of traits that may or may not be apt descriptions of you. Everything on this list is a characteristic that employers tend to value highly in employees. Interviewers may be looking for some of these qualities in addition to your job-specific skills and abilities, but no interviewer will expect anyone to have all of these traits.

WORKSHEET: YOUR TRAITS

- Creativity
- Innovativeness
- Curiosity
- Desire to learn
- Ambition
- Gumption
- Grit
- Ethical judgment
- Decisiveness
- Leadership
- Courageousness (willing to take measured risks)
- Adaptability
- Energy
- Self-confidence
- Self-reliance
- Loyalty
- Dependability
- Conscientiousness
- Integrity
- Honesty
- Trustfulness
- Humility

- Competitiveness
- Tactfulness
- Friendliness
- Team-orientation
- Goal-orientation
- Ability to work well under pressure or in high-stress situations
- Organizational skills
- Ability to locate and evaluate information
- Oral communication skills
- Written communication skills
- Reading comprehension skills
- Analytic ability
- Problem-solving ability
- Critical thinking ability
- Ability to transfer abstract knowledge to real-world situations
- Ability to work with people from diverse cultures and different backgrounds
- Knowledge of _____

- _____

- _____

- _____

WHAT TO DO WITH THE WORKSHEET

1. Go back to the lists that you created of things people do and do not think are true about you. If any work-related traits aren't included on the worksheet above, add them in the blank spaces. (Phrase them all positively, so that having the trait would be positive at work and not having the trait would be negative at work.) On the other blank lines, add any work-related skills, abilities, or content knowledge that you noticed throughout the other exercises. (You don't have to be an expert to claim

knowledge; you simply need to know the topic well relative to other people at your stage of life.)

2. Next, go through the worksheet above and put an asterisk (*) next to the traits or abilities at which you do *not* excel. These asterisks should go next to characteristics that are neither your strong skills nor your strengths relative to your peers. In other words, you don't think they are good descriptions of you, and people don't tend to say them about you.

3. Circle the traits, including the ones you added yourself, that are the *most* true of you. These are your strongest attributes. Anything that is circled is a strength that you should try to convey during your interviews.

4. Anything that is asterisked amounts to a weakness. Whether or not each weakness is brought up during the interview is up to you. However, you should identify at least one of your weaknesses that you could work to overcome. If it is something that is hard to change, think of strategies you can use to prevent this weakness from hurting your job performance.

FINISHING YOUR FOUNDATION

When you've completed the exercises above, you should have a well-developed sense of the foundation of your story. You've reflected on the path your education and career have taken so far, and why you want particular opportunities or experiences in your next job. You know when, where, and how you can be most successful in the future, based on your reflections on your past experiences.

In the space below, take a moment to gather together all of the information you worked through in this chapter. Look back through all of the exercises that you completed, and select only the most important facts—the ones that are fundamental to understanding who you are as a worker.

This is a summary of my general interview story:

I am a _____

_____ person who is

skilled at _____

_____ and has knowledge of

_____

_____. I want a job that

_____

_____, and I think I will fit best at organizations that

_____. For

an interviewer to understand who I am and what I will bring to

the job, it will be helpful for them to know _____

_____.

For help filling in your story, you can use the following prompts:

I am a [strongest work-related traits] person who is skilled at [skills, abilities] and has knowledge of [work-related knowledge]. I want a job that [values, interests, long-term plans and goals], and I think I will fit best at organizations that [values, characteristics of coworkers]. For an interviewer to understand who I am and what I will bring to the job, it will be helpful for them to know [overarching motives, lessons learned, facts that differ from my default story].

Keep in mind that this isn't your final and complete story. That's something you're going to need to develop further, with more specific details. To really excel at telling your story, you'll also need to tailor this version of your story for each specific job interview. We'll work on this in Chapters Eight and Ten.

SUMMARY

- Identifying the common themes in your life helps you to describe who you are as a worker to someone who doesn't know you (an interviewer).
- You can do this by thinking about your motives, turning points, highs and lows, how people talk about you, and the specific traits that you embody.

CHAPTER 8: ADDING STRUCTURE TO YOUR STORY

We already told you about the time Emily wasn't hired at the Olive Garden. It happened because she didn't tailor her story to the job.

After all, she had plenty of waitressing experience. She knew how to take orders, deliver food, and deal with customer complaints. What she didn't understand was what Olive Garden wanted in its wait staff. When the interviewer asked about her experiences as a server, he wanted to hear about how she upsold or treated tables with children differently than tables full of adults. Instead, she simply talked about how long she had been a server. When he asked why she wanted to move from her then employer to Olive Garden, he was probably looking for an interest in the brand; she just thought that she could earn more in tips. Looking back, the job might not have been a good fit for Emily—in part because she hadn't given much thought to how the job would differ from her current job. As Emily has since learned, you can't expect that your background—even if it's relevant—will make you a good job candidate; you need to give thought to how your background relates to each specific job.

HOW TO USE THIS CHAPTER

In the last chapter, you built the foundation of your interview story. Now it's time to add shape using specific details that will make sense in the context of your next job.

The exercises in this chapter are designed to help you prepare for a target interview for a particular job. If you've just begun applying for jobs and don't have a specific job interview you want to prepare for, go ahead and skip to the next chapter. You can come back to this chapter once you're ready.

If you interview for multiple jobs, you will go through this chapter multiple times. In doing so, you'll find that the exercises get easier and easier. Much of the time, the results will be similar. But sometimes, you'll find that the focus of your story needs to be tweaked, or that the content of your story needs to be communicated differently. This is natural. Each job has slightly different requirements, and each job involves working with different people. Repeating this chapter will help you to explain your story in these different contexts so that every interviewer understands what you will bring to their organization.

THE FRAMING WALLS OF YOUR INTERVIEW STORY

As you may have gathered from earlier chapters, your story is a broad picture of you, but its supporting structure comes from facts about you—your capabilities, interests, the traits that will help you fit in a particular organization, and the like. Remember, interviewers need to hear three things during your interview. They need to hear that: you have the skills, abilities, and knowledge necessary to do the job; you are interested in this particular job; and you will fit well with your future coworkers and the organization itself.

To do the activities in the rest of this chapter, you'll need to be thinking of a specific job. If you have an interview scheduled, that's great. Pull up the ad for that job. (If you didn't save a copy when you applied for the job and it's no longer posted, now you know—always save a copy! For the time being, find a handful of similar job ads and combine them into a single description that seems to capture what you remember of the job when you applied to it.) If you don't have any interviews scheduled yet but want to work through these activities anyway, use the job ad for one of the jobs you've applied to. Choose one that seems representative of the types of jobs you'll be interviewing for soon.

As an example, we're going to work through this ad for a teacher:

Elementary School Teacher

Springfield Public Schools is the fastest growing school district in the state. We are looking for highly motivated, energetic, tenacious teachers for the upcoming school year. Each of our schools provides a welcoming learning environment that encourages achievement in all students, regardless of their background, neighborhood, or English language skills. Our teachers work collaboratively to implement innovative, cross-department curricula that serve our diverse student population.

Duties: The incumbent will teach and facilitate adequate academic progress for sixth-grade students. Specific responsibilities include: preparing lesson plans, grading homework in a timely manner, and performing other duties as assigned.

Qualifications: Successful candidates must have a Bachelor's degree from an accredited college or university, a valid state teaching license, and excellent verbal and written communication skills. Experience as a classroom instructor preferred.

In addition to your job ad, you'll also need a piece of paper with a simple grid or a spreadsheet. You need enough room in each cell of the grid for a few words. We've provided an example below; you can also find a full version on our website, morethananswers.com.

YOUR SKILLS, KNOWLEDGE, AND ABILITIES

First, we'll work through the competencies you'll need to be able to talk about during the interview. Read through the job ad, paying particular attention to sections that describe the requirements of the job and the duties you would be asked to perform. You're looking for all of the specialized knowledge, skills, and abilities that appear in the ad. Write these competencies down in the left-most column of your grid, using one row for each competency. For the time being, you can ignore the rest of the columns. When you're done, your grid should look something like this:

Story element	Experience #1	Experience #2	Experience #3	...
Competency				
Lesson planning				
Time management				
Verbal communication skills				
Written communication skills				

Next, go through the list in your grid and put an asterisk next to all of the items that you do *not* excel at. These should include any characteristics that are neither your strongest skills nor your strengths relative to your peers. In other words, these items don't describe you well, and people don't mention them when they speak about you. (Sound familiar? Yup, these are just like the weaknesses that you identified in the previous chapter.)

Now flip back to your summary from the end of the previous chapter. If you see any items in your grid that also appears in your summary, circle them. These represent not only your strongest attributes but also attributes that are important for this specific job, and they are among the most important things to communicate clearly to an interviewer. You know they want these characteristics in an employee and you have them, so you need to make sure that the interviewer knows this.

Finally, look carefully at the traits that you marked with asterisks; these are not only weaknesses but very important weaknesses because they have the potential to affect your job performance. You may or may not be asked about these during the interview. However, you *must* put a plan in place to overcome these weaknesses because without one, you shouldn't expect to last in this job very long.

YOUR INTERESTS

Now that you've identified all of the core competencies needed for the job, it's time to consider how you can talk about your interest in the specific job. Take another pass through the job ad, again focusing on the duties and responsibilities. Which of these responsibilities make you most excited and why? What aspects of the job might keep you there for many years? Other interesting aspects of the job might be scattered throughout the rest of the ad; take time to re-read the whole thing.

Some of your interests might be really broad. For instance, you might be interested in the job because of the career field itself. You don't need to focus on these aspects unless they're not obvious. For instance, if your college degree was in elementary education, and you've applied to teach at an elementary school, it's pretty obvious that you're interested in teaching. But if you are *particularly* interested in some aspect of elementary education, like facilitating social development in pre-teens, that would be an interest to keep in mind as you think about constructing your story. Other interests may be unrelated to the career field, such as the chance to work with a particular computer operating system.

In a new sub-section in your grid labeled interests, take the time to list each of the things that you find interesting about the job. Your grid will now look something like this:

Story element	Experience #1	Experience #2	Experience #3	...
Competency				
Lesson planning				
Time management				
Verbal communication skills				
Written communication skills				
Interest				
Teaching pre-teens				
Working in a diverse environment				

YOUR FIT

The last of the elements that you need to consider when framing or adding structure to your story is fit. Your fit in an organization is pretty abstract. Your preparation for an interview should focus on two things. First, search for ways that your beliefs about the goals of your work are aligned with those of the organization. That is, think about which of your values are reflected in what the organization says about itself, what it does, and how it works. Second, look for ways that you are similar to current employees. These may be obvious (perhaps you attended the same school as half of the organization's employees) or less obvious (perhaps you have a work ethic that is similar to the one the organization says its employees have).

Now, turn to the job ad one last time. And while you're at it, go to the organization's website. (The organization's "careers" and "about us" pages are usually good places to start.) Which of your values do you see reflected in the way the organization or its employees are described? Does the mission of the organization align with the impact that you would like your career to have? For instance, is the organization striving to use technology to change the world, promote social justice, create high-quality products, entertain people and bring joy to their lives, preserve natural resources, foster innovation through investment, increase awareness of a particular issue, create knowledge through scientific discovery, cure illness, or provide people with pleasant environments to relax in? Believing in an organization's mission is a common and fundamental way to find your fit.

If the website describes specific employees, what do you have in common with these people? Do any share a similar background with you (e.g., where you grew up, went to school, previously worked)? How are the employees described in general? What looks familiar when you read about their work styles, work ethic, and individual personalities?

Once you identify the most important ways in which you fit with the organization and your potential coworkers, write these down in a third sub-section of your grid:

Story element	Experience #1	Experience #2	Experience #3	...
Competency				
Lesson planning				
Time management				
Verbal communication skills				
Written communication skills				
Interest				
Teaching pre-teens				
Working in a diverse environment				
Fit				
In my hometown				
Teachers are motivated & energetic				

Didn't think you could squeeze this much material from a job ad? This process takes time, but you'll be thankful for your preparation in the interview. Keep your grid handy. You'll fill in the blank cells as you read Chapter Ten.

THE FINISHED LAYOUT

Though many of the jobs that you have applied to and will apply to will require similar skills and fulfill similar interests, each job is indeed distinct. The ratio of the specific duties required of you may vary and the work environments will undoubtedly differ. Being able to describe why you are great for a specific job, rather than a generic job with the same title at a generic organization, will make the interviewer feel comfortable hiring you.

SUMMARY

- The skills, knowledge, and abilities that are among your most dominant traits and are necessary for a specific job are also the ones you should always talk about during an interview.
- Any skills, knowledge, and abilities necessary for the job that are not among your strengths are important weaknesses. You need to develop a plan to address these qualities.
- You can use information available in the job ad to identify features of the job that are appealing and then use these to communicate your interest in the job during the interview.
- You can talk about your fit with the organization by highlighting similarities between you and its employees, and between your values and the larger mission of the organization.

CHAPTER 9: DISTRACTIONS FROM YOUR STORY

So far, you have built a large portion of your story, and you've learned the ways in which building this story is like building a house. Both have a foundation, walls that provide structure and add character, and a roof that covers the building and joins together its various pieces.

The last stage of building your story is its roof, the examples that tie together all of the elements that you'll need to convey for a successful interview. But before we get to how to build this roof, we first want to talk about what your story *shouldn't* include.

DISTRACTIONS

Have you ever seen pictures from a real estate listing and thought, *wow, I can't believe anyone decorates their house like that*? Realtors often recommend that home sellers remove highly personal decorations like family pictures and paint walls in neutral colors. They give this advice because they know that bright green shag carpeting, cluttered piles of belongings, or a mural of the family painted on the living room wall can turn off potential buyers. Buyers have a hard time ignoring bold, individual styles, despite the fact that odd furniture and bizarre artwork will no longer be there once the place is sold.

This doesn't mean people shouldn't express themselves in their own homes; it simply means that, when it's time to sell these homes, people need to consider their broader goals. The same principle applies to job interviews. Talking about hard-to-understand or irrelevant personal details during your interview doesn't mean you won't be offered the job. After all, you may decide that you want a job in which the hiring manager appreciates the whole you, not just you as a worker. And sharing certain personal quirks may help show that you can fit into a quirky workplace. But if you want to increase the likelihood that your job search is brief and fruitful, you should avoid distracting your interviewers.

PAST, PRESENT, FUTURE

When Emily was nine years old, she wanted with all her heart to be a paleontologist. You probably know that most people don't grow up to be what they wanted to be as children. Without knowing anything else about Emily, it's not a stretch to guess that she is now something other than a paleontologist. That's because a great deal changes between childhood and adulthood. If all adults became what they wanted to be as children, we'd have a lot more princesses and professional basketball players.

Now, if *two* years ago—as an adult—Emily had desperately wanted to be a paleontologist, might the fact that she's nowhere near that career field seem a little stranger? Might you question whether she is able to have two career passions simultaneously, one that makes her productive and efficient at work, and another that she's fine simply dreaming about? These questions, which can and do distract interviewers, can arise because of uncertain associations between your past and your present.

Most interviewers would feel a little uncertain hiring an accountant who talks about recently wanting to be an archeologist. The reason? There is no sharp line between your past of two years ago and your present. Things that happened to you in middle school are relatively easy to ignore. Discontinuity between childhood and adulthood is reasonable, even expected. But things that happen in adulthood, especially within a few years of each other, are much harder to separate.

Let's look at another example, one that mixes up the present with an uncertain future. Charles spoke with Amber, a materials development chemist, during a mock interview. Earlier, she had given a very clear description of her daily duties as a chemist, and Charles wanted to know which of these duties she was most interested in continuing in her next job and which duties she was less enthusiastic about.

> Charles: What would your ideal job be? If you could sort of carve it out like, 'here's how I'd like to spend my day'?
>
> Amber: I'd actually like to open a bakery.
>
> Charles: A bakery?
>
> Amber: I'm in culinary school right now at night and I bake for the farmer's market. Ideally, in like twenty or thirty years, I'll probably open a bakery.

With our career coach hats on, we loved this answer. It was a great example of someone working toward a long-term goal. But as interviewers, Amber's answer made us cringe. Even though Amber wasn't planning to start the bakery for some time, her plans called into question whether she actually wanted the job to which she had applied. How long would she stick around in this job? Would she really be willing to wait *twenty years* to open her own shop, or was she looking for a job to pay the bills while she finished culinary school, with the intention to quit once her farmer's market wares started to garner local press?

We honestly don't know Amber's intentions. We don't know whether twenty years was a truthful estimate, or whether it was said in order to cover up the fact that she knew that a desire to open a bakery might sound weird to a hiring manager for a job in chemistry. And frankly, it doesn't matter: what matters is whether the interviewer believes there is a real difference between the present (the person who will work hard as a chemist) and the future (the bakery owner).

If there isn't a real difference, which Amber will show up to work? Will Baker Amber ask to leave early three times a week in order to get to culinary school? Will Baker Amber spend time finding new recipes online while she's supposed to be inventing new formulas for plastics? A hiring manager might luck out and get Chemist Amber all day, every day. But if the hiring manager has any doubt about whether these two very different people are indeed separated by a significant amount of time, neither Amber is likely to get the job.

The past and the future can become a distraction from your story if they are inconsistent with who you are now. Luckily, this is not a problem for everyone. If you found your ideal career path early in life, you shouldn't have a problem talking about and connecting your past, present, and future. But if you have changed in some substantive way, or if you plan to change in the future, you'll need to be very clear and careful about how you talk about these changes, or leave them unsaid altogether.

One great way to persuasively illustrate a change like these is to assign that change a trigger. Eric, the international human rights lawyer, might have done this by intentionally bringing up the anecdote of the *favelas* in Rio de Janeiro. That was the moment when he started to change from someone who didn't know what he wanted to do with his life (other than travel) and became someone who felt a drive to help people who live in poverty. There was a lot more involved in Eric's path: he had to take the LSAT, apply to schools, get his legal education, and pass the bar. But even if this trigger wasn't the only important event in his transformation, it was an event with strong explanatory power.

PERSONAL DETAILS

We talked about hiding your personal photos when selling your home, but you may want to mention some elements of your personal life during your interview when these elements are important for the narrative. This is especially true when you don't have a lot of examples to draw upon from previous employment. But always remember that your interview story should be focused on who you are as a worker. Never include irrelevant details that detract from this message.

Your story ends once you have included enough detail to explain who you would be if you were indeed hired. If your background is identical to the background of most people in the job—perhaps you went to the same college, got the same degree, and have the same career aspirations as the majority of your future coworkers—then your story is very straightforward. But if your background is less conventional, you may need to include a few personal details that help the interviewer to piece together why you are seeking this particular job.

Throughout your interview, you need to tell a consistent story. A consistent story never confuses an interviewer. The interviewer will have a good sense of who you are after reading your resume and cover letter, and your answers in the interview should be harmonized with what they have surmised. Don't make the interviewer think that you're bubbly, sociable, and a great fit for a client-relations position, and then casually throw in the fact that you like to take walks alone at 3 a.m. Middle-of-the-night solitary walks don't fit with most people's view of a person who is good at relating to people and earning their accounts.

RED FLAGS

Another form of distraction is the *red flag*. A red flag is anything that seems to suggest (whether rightly or wrongly) that you might not be an ideal employee. Showing up late to an interview is a red flag. Red flags also include saying something totally unexpected, something that introduces uncertainty into the mind of the interviewer. Comments like this make the interviewer question whether you are truly able to do the job, whether you actually want the job, whether you might be a troublemaker, or whether you are being honest. If the interviewer thinks, *I'm not sure whether this person would really fit in here* or asks themselves, *can I be sure that this person is really capable of handling the job?*, you will have gone from being a strong candidate to being a candidate that they may not want to risk hiring. Even if all of your other qualifications and alignment with the job are perfect, if you present an unresolved red flag, you may very well hinder your chances of getting a job offer.

Common red flags include mental and physical illnesses or disabilities, family obligations, past arrests, having been fired or laid off, critiques about a former employer, strong personality traits (e.g., risk-taking or argumentativeness), or even just talking about a desire to go to graduate school. These absolutely aren't things to be ashamed of or things that you should try to hide. If you're asked about one of these topics, you should be honest. Then, you should explain to the best of your ability why this issue doesn't matter—in short, why it won't affect your job performance. And if you're not asked about an issue like these, you don't need to bring it up during an interview. Keep in mind that things that sometimes seem innocuous, things that you might talk about casually because you know that they don't reflect poorly on you, can be red flags if they aren't explained well enough to be understood by the interviewer.

We're not saying that you should never talk about those topics, or about anything else in your story that might sound like a red flag. We're simply saying that you need to be aware that some aspects of your life outside of work may be misconstrued or may give someone the wrong impression. If you describe your devotion to your family, you need to simultaneously describe how you balance that devotion with your duty to work. If you want to show how you overcame an addiction, you need to do so in a way that makes it clear that you're not at risk for a relapse. An interviewer's job is to find and hire an employee who will work at the level expected by the organization. As long as you can do that, there is no need to give the interviewer any doubt.

DON'T RAISE RED FLAGS UNTIL IT'S TIME

The idea of not distracting an interviewer from the message of your story doesn't mean that you have to avoid talking about something that is important to you. Instead, it means that you should convey information that might raise uncertainties in a way that minimizes those uncertainties.

Timing is important: raised too soon, red flags may take you out of the running entirely, while issues raised too late may diminish your chances of negotiation for the right accommodations.

Hypothetical job seeker James, for instance, is looking for a full-time job. He is also a caregiver for his mom, who has early-stage dementia along with other health problems. He knows that she doesn't deal well with change or variable schedules, and because he can't afford round-the-clock care, he wants to make sure that whatever job he takes never requires late nights or more than forty hours a week. A home health aide comes to the house during the day, but he needs to be available to take his mom to occasional medical appointments. His job needs to be flexible enough that he can miss an hour here or there. How can he ensure that the jobs he interviews for are right for him without raising a red flag?

To begin, James should not mention the issue too soon. That means not talking about the fact that he takes care of his mother during the bulk of the interview. James should provide many examples of the quality of his work and how dedicated he is to being a good employee. Once he has conveyed the part of his story that is centered on his skills, abilities, and attitude, he might ask a question like, "Could you tell me what a typical employee's work schedule is like?" Or, "How often should I expect to arrive early or stay late?" These are reasonable questions that many people want to ask, as the answers help them to envision their lives within the organization.

These questions are useful because they don't get into James's particular situation, yet their answers communicate a lot about the culture of the organization and its attitude toward work hours. In general, an organization that requires most employees to work overtime or be in the office during specific hours isn't going to be the type of organization where James can succeed and feel good about his job—even if he were able to negotiate more flexibility for himself because of his situation. Unless James is *asked* why he wants to know the answers to these questions (and he probably won't be), he doesn't need to go into detail about why he wants to know these things. He'll get the impression he needs without forcing the interviewer to question whether James has the time and energy for the job.

Once James has made his case that he be hired, the best time to make a request for flexibility in his schedule is after he has been offered the job and before he has accepted it. At that time, it's totally appropriate to provide a reason for a request that deviates from the norm: his mom has frequent medical appointments, and he needs to transport her to these appointments and be there with her. The employer may not be able to accommodate his request, but at least James will have made this request from a strong position and know that he tried his best.

GROWING FROM EXPERIENCE

At this point, you may have the sense that we advocate for a way of thinking about the job interview that is different from many other career experts. Many people will try to convince you to turn weaknesses into strengths, or to sidestep sticky issues. Their advice sounds something like this:

> If you're asked how long you've been unemployed and it's been a while, don't give the interviewer a specific time period. Instead, say, "Time doesn't factor into my job search because I've been looking for the right fit."

> If you're asked whether you would rather work alone or in a team, say, "I've found that I can be productive in both settings."

> If you're asked about your weaknesses, say, "I'm a perfectionist. My attention to detail means sometimes I care too much about a project, and I have to work longer hours to make sure it's perfect."

All of these answers are rubbish, and interviewers know it. Evasiveness is a distraction. If you aren't being genuine with some of your answers, interviewers will question whether they can trust anything else you say. Furthermore, any well-trained interviewer will follow-up your sidestepping answer with a more probing question, leaving you to awkwardly answer their original question anyway.

When we met with Jeremy, he had been unemployed for several months. He was getting desperate. He did, however, have an upcoming interview for a great job, and he wanted our help explaining why he had been out of work for so long. He could have easily found himself having the following conversation while he tried not to say that he had resigned because his employer had given him the choice of resigning or being fired:

> Interviewer: Why did you leave your last job?
>
> Jeremy: I wanted to seek other opportunities. I'm looking for a job that allows me to capitalize on my ten years of outstanding retail management experience and grow with a dynamic company, like yours.
>
> Interviewer: And I see from your resume you've been out of work now for the last nine months. So, did you resign, or were you fired or laid off?
>
> Jeremy: I resigned.

If Jeremy had said this, the interviewer might think that he was impulsive and had a hard time engaging in long-term planning. After all, Jeremy could very well have sought "other opportunities" while he was employed. For certain jobs, this misperception might not be a deal breaker. For many jobs however, impulsivity and poor planning skills are undesirable traits. In addition, these qualities may not be consistent with the rest of the story that Jeremy was trying to tell the interviewer.

If you learn to tell your story well, you won't find yourself in a conversation that somehow makes you seem like someone you're not, or worse, someone who is dishonest. It's the difference between thinking, *Hey, maybe I can pull one over on this interviewer and get the job anyway!* and thinking, *I've grown from that experience, and I want to work with people who value growth, so I can be honest because the interviewer will appreciate and understand my story.*

Instead of trying to avoid the question, Jeremy used his story and answered the interviewer this way:

> Interviewer: Why did you leave your last job?
>
> Jeremy: I thought I could make the transition from ten successful years managing people to a product management position. But it turns out the skill sets are more different than I thought, and I just didn't have the necessary skills. I wasn't happy there, and they weren't happy with my performance. What I've learned from that experience is that I should be managing people. It's what I'm good at, and it's what I enjoy doing most. Now I'm looking for a job that allows me to capitalize on my experience and grow with a dynamic company like yours.

In this version, it was clear to the interviewer that Jeremy wasn't trying to hide anything. His answer was open and better, it made sense; it didn't distract from his story. He demonstrated that he had reflected on his tough experiences, learned from them, and was ready to do a great job. This type of growth from experience is exactly what a good interviewer wants to hear. It also happens to be a good way to be a better employee.

Just like tacky furniture and wallpaper can distract homebuyers, personal details can distract interviewers from your overall story. Whenever possible, you should pick examples from your life that are easy to explain, easy to understand, and that tie your story together.

SUMMARY

- When describing things about yourself that have changed recently or will change, take a moment to clearly explain the change and who you are right now.
- Your story is not your memoir. It does not need to include personal details that are irrelevant to your work performance and career trajectory.
- If you think that part of your story might make an interviewer doubt your ability to do the job well, leave it out of the interview

or carefully explain why that issue won't impede your performance.

- If you need flexibility or specific accommodations from an employer, the best time to ask for these is during negotiations, not during the interview.
- You can be open and honest about parts of your story that sound less-than-desirable once you're capable of explaining how you learned from the experience. Good interviewers look for employees who can learn from mistakes.

CHAPTER 10: THE FINAL TOUCHES

In Chapter Eight, you identified your strengths and weaknesses, your key interests, and the ways that you might fit with various organizations. These are important components of your story, but they do not complete it.

It's not enough to tell an interviewer, "I'm perfect for this job" or even, "I'm perfect for this job because I'm motivated and energetic." You need to convince the interviewer that these things are in fact true. Providing the interviewer with sufficient details to hold your story together is the equivalent of putting a roof over your house. A house without a roof isn't much of a home at all. A job candidate may be able to talk like they know how to do good work, but without examples that fill in the gaps, most interviewers won't be convinced.

When Charles gave Riya a mock interview, he asked her what strengths she had relative to the other students in her classes. Riya said that she had strong leadership skills. But she didn't just ask Charles to believe her; she spontaneously continued by telling him that she'd just been elected chair of a student association and that she attributed her election to the fact that other students had recognized her leadership skills. This was a fantastic example because it gave Charles a reason to believe that other people agree with Riya's assessment of herself. (Riya's example was also great because it showed that she seeks out opportunities to use and further develop these leadership skills.)

Like Riya, you ought to be able to convince an interviewer to believe what you say about yourself. To do this, start by looking through your resume. Using the grid that you started in Chapter Eight, add titles to the top of each column. These titles should include every job, activity, and educational experience that appears on your resume. Leave a column to the right for other experiences in case you need it later.

Once you've done this, try to think of an example for each cell. (You can leave cells in the "other" column blank as long as at least one of the cells in the row is filled in to your satisfaction.) When you're finished, your grid should look something like this:

Story element	Student teaching	Summer camp job	College classes	Other: not on resume
Competency				
Lesson planning	Planned and led lessons on Neptune, Oregon Trail, multiplying fractions	Planned and led outdoor activities	Learned to start with objectives, then develop activities, and include checks for under-standing	
Time management	Observed lead teacher's techniques	Used calendar app to schedule activities for each day	Used active reading and notetaking strategies to balance courses with clubs	
…				

EXAMPLES OF SKILLS, KNOWLEDGE, ABILITIES

Examples that best illustrate your competencies should include events or positions in which you demonstrated those skills. Ideally, your examples will be relatively specific and showcase the fact that you are effective (e.g., you completed a certain project, you were successful in performing a specific task, or you are currently making progress toward a new achievement).

In the example grid above, the job seeker includes three very different examples of time management. One demonstrates that he adopted specific, efficient studying skills so that he could do well in his classes while also participating in several student groups. That is, he had multiple goals that might be hard to reach simultaneously, so he identified strategies that allowed him to make the best use of his time. Another example involves a strategy that he used as a camp counselor: in order to keep track of the timing of meals, camp-wide events, and small group activities, he used a scheduling app on his phone. This ensured that he was never late for any of his duties. And finally, when he was student teaching, he was largely on the schedule of his lead teacher and didn't find much opportunity to implement his own strategies. He did however observe the teacher using a color-coded set of folders to keep her paperwork organized, and he now plans to use the same system to make sure that he has his paperwork sorted and prioritized.

Be sure not to skip over any required competencies that you noted as weaknesses. If you're asked about these weaknesses, you'll need to have an example that you can use to address that weakness. Try to find a time when you tried to use each skill, even if it didn't work out. Then think about how you would approach that problem or task differently in the future. Your plans to overcome or mitigate your weaknesses should be part of your answer.

EXAMPLES OF INTERESTS

In the interests section, your examples should be focused on demonstrating how you in fact know that these are your interests. If you're drawn to a particular task that you will get to do in a prospective job, an example might be the first time that you did that task, with a description of how fun you found it. Or you might describe one of your greatest achievements.

Josh wanted a job as a real estate agent. When he spoke with Charles, however, he was working as a leasing agent for an apartment complex. When Charles asked him why he was interested in real estate, Josh said that he liked the challenge of finding someone the perfect home. His answer ended there, and Josh missed an opportunity to ensure that he convinced Charles of his interest. Josh might have supported his statement by relaying a story of doing just that with a prospective tenant, such as working with a woman who had particular desires for the size and layout of her new home and who also had a strict budget. An example like this would have demonstrated how his interest in working with clients will carry over to his next job in real estate.

EXAMPLES OF FIT

Just like your interests, the examples you identify about your fit with the organization and the job should articulate why you know these things to be true. You might start by thinking about times in your life when you were in a similar environment (whether in a job or not), and then talk about how great those experiences were. You might describe situations in which you had the opportunity to work with people who are like the organization's current employees, and discuss how smoothly that went.

This involves adapting your response to the work environment. If you're seeking a job at a company that describes itself as having a collaborative environment with a flat structure, you'll want to identify examples that involve teamwork. You'll want to focus on experiences that you've had working with people who have more (or less) experience and skill than you. You'll want to talk about the ways in which you develop rapport with coworkers and how you've cooperated with others to create successful results. In this case, these examples are more important to highlight than other experiences in which you were the star of the show or completed projects independently.

When Ryan was applying for a job in New York with a company based in England, we helped him make a case for his fit in a way that distinguished him from other candidates. Ryan quickly mentioned during the interview that he had been born in England to British parents and had become a US citizen as a teenager. This helped the interviewers learn that Ryan understands British customs and idioms; this meant that it wouldn't be hard for him to actively contribute to overseas conference calls. Ryan also mentioned that he visits his cousins and other family in England once a year. Some people get nervous traveling to foreign countries and navigating new airports; Ryan mentioned his travel experience to signal that if the job required international travel, he was comfortable with it. The job did in fact require travel, and now Ryan has the chance to see his family more often, while the company pays for his flights.

To demonstrate your fit with a particular organization, you can also pay attention to the way that you present yourself. This is one of the reasons that your attire matters. Who do you think would show better fit for a job at a tattoo parlor: someone who wears a T-shirt to show off the designs on their own arms, or someone who shows up in a suit with a conservative haircut and no visible piercings? Both might be highly skilled artists who are interested in helping customers to express themselves, but the first applicant looks like they belong, while the second seems like an outsider. Wear clothes that show that you know what the real professionals wear, whatever industry you happen to be in.

OTHER EXAMPLES

If you get to the end of your resume and can't find a good example of an experience in which you demonstrated a particular skill, a time when you came to understand one of your interests, a time when your motivations were reinforced, or a way to show that you fit with the organization, think beyond the piece of paper in front of you. Your resume is just a starting point for the interview. You can always talk about jobs that didn't make the cut (like a part-time job in high school), a scouting project, or even a family vacation. Add these types of examples to the "other" column if one of your rows is lacking.

FINISHING YOUR STORY

The examples that you identified as you worked through this chapter should be your go-to answers in the interview. You can mention other examples, but whenever possible, these examples are the content you want to talk about. The more similarity and consistency there is in your examples and answers, the more confident the interviewer will be that you are the worker you say you are.

Depending on how diverse your interests and skills are, the list of things that you need to communicate in a given interview may sound quite a bit different than the summary of your story that you composed at the end of Chapter Seven. Even if this list and your story summary overlap perfectly, you'll need to incorporate your fit into your story. Therefore, the very last step in building your story is to put all of its pieces together.

Take a look once more at the summary that you wrote at the end of Chapter Seven. If you need to highlight additional (or different) traits, skills, or interests, make those changes here. You can also add more specific information about how you fit with the organization in question. This second summary is your story for the specific job for which you're about to interview.

This is a summary of my specific interview story:

I am a _____

_____ person who is

skilled at _____

_____ and has knowledge of

_____

_____ . I want a job that

_____

_____ , and I think I will fit at this organization because

_____ . For an

interviewer to understand who I am and what I will bring to the

job, it will be helpful for them to know _____

_____ .

When you're done with everything in this chapter and the previous chapters, you should have a well-developed story. You should be able to explain the path that your education and career have taken so far, as well as why you want particular opportunities or experiences in your next job. Your story should be tailored to the specific job you're interviewing for, and it should also include specific examples. You now know *what* to communicate (the most important traits, skills, interests, and ways that you fit) and *how* to communicate it (evidence from your past). Each of the components of your story now works together to complement and support the others and to represent you as a great candidate for the job.

SUMMARY

- Examples help interviewers believe that you know yourself well and that what you say about yourself is accurate.
- Every element of your story that you want to communicate during an interview should be illustrated by examples from your work history, work-related experiences, or other experiences, if necessary.

CHAPTER 11: PERFECT TAKES PRACTICE

Having a story and knowing where it ends will almost certainly make you more prepared, but it doesn't guarantee a knockout interview. Knockout interviews come with practice. If you take the time to practice your story, you will go further than most other job seekers. They will be winging it during their interviews, and they'll miss opportunities to present their best qualities. They may also accidently describe themselves in ways that distract or confuse their interviewers. You won't make those mistakes because you will have practiced what to say and when to say it.

WAYS TO PRACTICE

Early in their careers, pretty much everyone can benefit from these methods of interview practice, and we recommend that you do them all, in order, if you have time. No matter where you are in your career or your past success with interviews, practice will make you better.

STRATEGY 1. FIND EXAMPLE QUESTIONS

You can start by writing down common job interview questions that might be asked for almost any job. (We've listed a slew of these questions on our website, morethananswers.com.) Common questions often concern the basic facts of your work history and education, soft skills that are useful across careers and industries, your motivations, and your plans for the future.

After you've compiled this initial list, add more questions. Some job interviews will include highly technical questions, exercises in problem solving, or demonstrations of your skills. Whatever type of interview is most common to the jobs you are looking for, you should be able to find information about the types of questions most employers will ask. For instance, if you're going into graphic design, you should expect to be asked about design principles ("How do you use color?"). An interview for a sales position will typically require a demonstration of selling techniques ("How does our product compare to other products on the market?"). An interviewer for a more analytic position may ask you to exhibit knowledge of statistics ("What's a p-value?").

In addition to questions that are common to different types of jobs, you can often find questions that are specific to individual organizations. For a while, Google was famous for asking questions like, "What would you do if you were suddenly the size of a nickel and in a blender?" (If you don't know the answer to that one, have no fear. Google's current policy is to avoid asking those types of questions.) As of press time, Glassdoor.com and Quora.com are great sources for questions that have been asked during real interviews, listed by organization and role.

This strategy serves as a foundation for all of the other strategies, but if it's the only thing you have time for, it's still useful. The process of thinking through the different questions that an interviewer may ask will start to help you to prepare. But if you have more time, keep working through at least one of the additional strategies below.

STRATEGY 2. WRITE DOWN A FEW ANSWERS

In Chapter Ten, you already identified some of the core examples or details that you'll want to mention in your interview. Nevertheless, as you gathered example questions in Strategy 1 (above), you probably noticed topics for which you don't yet have examples. In this step, you'll identify more examples and think about how your best examples can be tapped to answer several questions.

Start by picking ten different types of behavioral ("tell me about a time when…") or situational questions ("what would you do if…") from the list that you generated in Strategy 1. Write one of these questions on a piece of paper. Below that, or to the side of it, start a two-column list. One column will include ways that you could answer the question, such as examples from your classes, jobs, or activities. The other column should be qualities about you that the example conveys.

If you use a grid, it will end up looking something like this:

Question	Example	Qualities
Tell me about a time when you delegated responsibility.	Class project, identified each task and made assignments for teammates	Leadership, understanding of task/business needs, strategic decision-making
	Led team during internship, let people switch roles throughout summer to learn all aspects of the work	Leadership, management of people

If you come up with more than one example that you could use to answer the question, we suggest using the example that best highlights the qualities most aligned with the rest of your story.

Your examples don't have to be complete anecdotes with a beginning and an end. For instance, in response to the question, "Can you tell me about a time when you demonstrated critical thinking skills?" you might reply by describing what you did on a daily basis at your last job, if that work was relevant.

If you're still stumped, you can try a more systematic approach. Start by reading through your resume to spark your memory. Think about your experiences within each job (paid or unpaid) and student group or activity that you have listed. Do any of these experiences give you a relevant answer to the question?

As you think through each piece of your resume, you will probably find yourself thinking, *that might be a good example to talk about in an interview* and maybe even, *I should avoid talking about that.* These thoughts run right into the next step: we now want you to think about how each of these experiences aligns with your story. You can begin by taking note of the examples that you believe are the best representations of your story. The best examples are the ones that are clearest (that is, the ones that you're able to tell succinctly) as well as most representative of the main themes of your story or the personal characteristics that you most want to portray. Even if the qualities they illustrate aren't the ones that you identified in your tailored story, some may be more or less consistent with your story than others.

Let's get even more specific. You can probably think of an example of conflict in each of your jobs or activities, maybe in some of your classes too. Some of these experiences involved minor conflict. Others might have been major conflicts. Which of these conflicts were you best able to deal with? Which one is a good reflection of how you hope to deal with conflicts in the future? Which experience taught you how to deal with conflicts more effectively? One of these examples will be the best one to highlight, and it won't necessarily be the first one that comes to mind. If you wait until the middle of a nerve-wracking interview to think of an example of a time in which you had to deal with conflict, you might blurt out the one that was easiest to remember. Unfortunately, the most memorable example is likely the most severe example, or the one with the worst ending. Instead of having to think on your feet, you should now be armed with an honest example of a time you dealt with conflict that is a true reflection of the employee you will strive to be at your next place of employment.

USING STARS TO MAKE EXAMPLES CLEAR

It's often said that past behavior predicts future behavior. With this in mind, some interviewers like to ask questions about job seekers' past behavior. These often start with something like "Tell me about a time when…" or "Describe a situation in which…."

These questions are best answered by giving background information that explains exactly what you did and then describing the outcome. You can use the acronym STAR to remember the things you need to include in your answers to behavioral questions like these.

Start by giving the interviewer some background about the **situation**. Communicate things like which job you were in when the example occurred, who the key people in the story are, and so forth. Then move on to describe the **task**: what was the specific problem you had to solve, the conflict you had to resolve, or the process you wanted to improve? For simple examples, you may be able to summarize both the situation and the task in a single sentence.

After you've described the situation and the task, you can then move on to the **action** itself. What did you do? Who did you consult with, how did you come to your decision, what approach did you take to this issue? Finally, be sure to tell the interviewer the **result** of your action. If possible, quantify the result. Otherwise, describe the lasting impact that your action had for the organization. If the result was negative (e.g., your solution didn't work, wasn't adopted, or wasn't well received by clients), make sure to wrap up your answer in a positive way by describing what you learned from this example and what would do differently in a future situation. That's all part of the result as well.

STRATEGY 3. SAY YOUR ANSWERS OUT LOUD

We can't stress this enough: thinking of your answers in your head is *not* the same as answering questions out loud. When you think through your answers in your head, words come fast. Once you start turning those thoughts into physical movements with your mouth, however, the answers will be much slower. You may add a lot of *ums, you knows,* or other filler sounds that don't make it into the soundtrack in your head and don't communicate your point. You'll also find yourself needing to think about how to phrase things so that they are very clear. Practicing your answers out loud helps you to find your timing, pacing, and delivery and makes these as smooth as possible. This strategy is particularly great if you are a little shy or socially anxious, or if you've never interviewed before and don't want to look like a fool in front of anyone.

The trick is not to repeat this method of practice too many times, especially with the same small set of example questions. You don't want to develop and memorize the perfect answers to each of your questions. Why not? Even a well-cultivated list of questions probably won't cover everything you'll be asked during the interview. In all likelihood, you'll receive questions you didn't plan for; a few memorized answers can leave you with an inconsistent performance. Furthermore, practicing too much makes people sound scripted. And sounding scripted can make the interviewer think they aren't getting to know the *real* you, the you who will be answering questions off the cuff as soon as you're hired.

STRATEGY 4. GET A LITTLE HELP

You don't have to go through this alone! Another way to practice is to have a friend, family member, or job coach pick questions from the long list that you made in Strategy 1. (They may even have their own questions to add to your list.) Ask your helper to read each question out loud, and then practice giving them your answer.

This strategy is great for two reasons. First, you'll be answering questions while also sitting and moving like you will during the interview. You'll have a chance to practice shaking hands across a table, maintaining eye contact, sitting with good posture, and looking professional throughout the interview. If you've never interviewed before, it can be nice to go through the process once in order to feel that you know what to expect.

The second benefit to practicing with someone else is that it gives you a chance to receive feedback on your answers. Don't expect too much from this feedback: your practice partner will probably try to say mostly nice things, and they may or may not know what interviewers are looking for when they hire. But if your helper knows you well, they may be able to suggest alternative answers that highlight your skills and knowledge better than the examples that you've chosen. And any attentive partner should be able to tell you if your answers seem cohesive and convincing.

For these reasons, we actually recommend doing practice interviews with several different people. Ideally, one of your mock interviewers would be with someone who is well versed in hiring and career coaching. Your college's career center may have free or low-cost sessions available, and this can be a great resource to use. The second of your mock interviewers would ideally be someone who knows you very well. The feedback you will receive from these people will be different, but both types of feedback are valuable. Your comfort level in the mock interview will likely be different too. You may be more or less stressed by talking to a stranger than you are by talking to a good friend, and these different environments can be good practice for the actual interview as well.

STRATEGY 5. FILM IT

We have one final suggestion. Whether you've chosen to practice by yourself or with someone else, videotape yourself and watch the video afterwards. (It doesn't have to be high quality; you can use your phone or even a web camera.)

By watching yourself, you'll be able to critique your own answers rather than rely simply on feedback from someone who wants to be nice. You'll also pick up on important details like whether you are speaking loudly enough, whether your answers are too long, and how enthusiastic you seem.

It can feel awkward to watch yourself talk, but don't let this stop you from watching your practice session. In order to make this process easier, we recommend a few tactics. The key is to avoid being so critical of yourself that you can't watch the whole video. You can pick and choose among the strategies below to find one that works for you.

First, think about watching the video with a kind and compassionate friend. The person who served as your mock interviewer is often a great choice because that person has already heard your answers and knows how the interview went. Turn on the video, joke with your friend about yourself for the first five minutes, and then rewind. Start from the beginning and watch the whole video to make sure that you're catching everything that you can.

If you prefer to watch in privacy, there are some other strategies you can use to make the experience easier. When Emily watches herself, she likes pretending that it isn't her on the video, although most people report this to be a difficult task. You can also watch the video first with the goal of writing down only the good things that you said or did. Once you've watched the video and identified those things, then go back and write down the things that you could improve on. Yet another strategy is to listen to the video once with your eyes closed, noticing just the content of your answers, before you watch it for a second time.

Finally, if all else fails, make more videos. No, seriously. Film yourself doing a few things that feel less important than the mock interview. This might include reading a grocery list, talking about your pet, or describing a vacation you want to take. Watch these videos over and over until you become more comfortable seeing and hearing yourself on camera. *Then* go back to the practice interview video. It should be easier to pay attention to what you're saying, now that you're more used to hearing the sound of your voice and seeing your facial expressions.

WHAT PRACTICE ACCOMPLISHES

At this point, you should have a good sense of what to convey in your interview and well as how to convey it. As a reminder, these things include your skills and knowledge, why you want the job, and your fit with the organization. You also need to convey these elements of your story in a way that shows that you're self-aware, and you need to share examples of these qualities in order to provide the interviewer with evidence. Ideally, you will also spend time reiterating the main points of your story. When the interviewer hears you say, "I put in the extra hours needed to make sure the project was completed on time" after you already called yourself hard-working, it reinforces this main theme and provides a concrete example that the interviewer can remember. Mentally, if not physically, the interviewer will be nodding along with you, affirming that your answers are reasonable and are indeed what they expect from someone like you. This makes the interviewer feel comfortable that they can predict how you will be in the future—when you are an employee of the organization.

To put it simply, practicing is *the best way* to make sure you are communicating everything you want to say and doing so clearly and accurately.

SUMMARY

- In a good interview, your story provides a coherent and consistent impression of who you are in every answer to every question.
- Practicing answers to a variety of questions is particularly important because it allows you to become accustomed to communicating your story with brief and clear examples.
- Good ways to practice include talking to yourself, talking with someone else, and evaluating video of yourself talking.

CHAPTER 12: BEYOND CONTENT

The content of your answers is by far the most important thing to practice before an interview. But once you've worked out your story, determined which examples are the best ones for you to draw upon during your answers, and practiced saying these answers out loud, there are other things you can do to polish your skills even further. In particular, it can be useful to think about how *much* you are communicating in each of your answers. Over the course of the whole interview, answers should be neither too long nor too short. Your answers need to be specific, but not so specific that you communicate inflexibility when you don't mean to.

ANSWERS THAT ARE TOO LONG

Charles was talking to Brittany, a college student who was hoping to land a summer internship in international trade and investment. He wanted to know about an internship that she had held the previous summer. There wasn't much detail about this internship on her resume, so he wasn't sure what she had learned or accomplished, and more importantly, he didn't know whether that experience was relevant to what she wanted to do in the future.

Charles asked Brittany to tell him about the internship and the organization, which was an educational testing company based in Iowa. Brittany's response was, like many of her previous answers, very conversational:

> It's very interesting, and it's across the street from another testing company. Iowa City is like an educational hub in terms of testing, and a lot of national tests come from Iowa City. But yeah, my dad lives there and I kind of grew up there, my parents got divorced when I was young and so I went back there every summer and they—my family—really wanted me—I'm the oldest—and so they wanted me to come back. And so I came back to see my brothers and sisters and before I got into that company I had to do a dining job which was just absolutely horrible. But yeah, that was...

She started to trail off, as if she'd forgotten what she was talking about, so Charles brought her back to the internship. "So what did you do there?"

> What I did there, I started off testing. They hire people for temp jobs and it was very strange because I was the youngest person there by like twenty years and they were mostly retired professors and so that was really cool. I was sitting beside a retired engineering professor and a retired statistical professor....

More than three minutes later, Charles had learned a lot about what this company does. But very little of Brittany's answer actually focused on what *she* had done, and none of it connected what she had learned in that internship with the very different type of internship that she wanted in the future. There were a few issues with her answer, but the biggest problem was that it was too long.

We recommend trying to keep your answers short. Most common interview questions can be answered in a minute, and many take much less time than that. It's not that your answer needs to be so short that you sound closed-off and evasive, or so brief that you fail to set up the situation and provide the result of your action. Here and there, it might take two minutes to give a strong, full answer. But in general, try to trim extraneous details and avoid minutes of monologue. There are four reasons to do this.

The first is pretty obvious: if you talk too long, the interviewer may lose interest or get distracted. And if they don't listen to what you're saying, there is no point in saying it.

The second reason is that the interviewer might start to think that you're long-winded. Your interviewer has blocked off a portion of time in their day to spend with you, and they have other work to get done when that time is over. If they are worried that you might talk all day long, they will sometimes limit their questions. Or they won't ask for clarification about something they didn't understand because they need to move on to cover their main questions.

This leads us to the third reason. You need to make sure that the interviewer has enough time to ask *all* of their most important questions. If a hiring manager is choosing between two candidates, they want to be able to compare these candidates to each other. They might ask twenty questions of the first job candidate, but only make it through ten of those questions with a more long-winded interviewee. If that happens, the candidate whose answers are too long will be at a disadvantage. The interviewer knows what they want to know about the first job candidate. The long-winded candidate, however, remains partly unknown. The interviewer will not be able to feel comfortable hiring that person because they just don't know that person well enough. When given the choice between a known and an unknown, the interviewer will usually either hire the candidate who is well-known (if their answers were satisfactory), or they will move on to interviewing other candidates. An interviewer is highly unlikely to bring back a long-winded candidate for an additional interview just so that they can finish their original list of questions.

The fourth reason not to give answers that are too long is that it is beneficial to keep your answers on point. Many people who give long answers to interview questions do so because they ramble. They tell tangential stories, they give too many details, or they change the topic of questions entirely. You should always strive to give the interviewer the information they are looking for—and no more. In Brittany's case, her family history and the age of her coworkers were examples of providing irrelevant information that pulled her away from her story.

In our research, we've also noticed that red flags are most abundant in the rambling portions of answers, usually those answers that weren't sufficiently planned ahead of time. Brittany wrapped up her answer by conveying positivity and an enjoyment of her work. Yet she slipped away from that persona at the beginning of her answer when she casually mentioned that another job had been "absolutely horrible." That gaffe begged a follow-up question about this horrible job, which wasn't even on her resume and therefore would never have been discussed if she hadn't brought it up.

HOW TO STOP TALKING

You know whether you tend to talk a lot. You also know whether you talk more when you're nervous. If you're concerned about being too chatty during an interview, there are several strategies you can use.

For long-winded people, your interview practice should including practicing your answers with a timer. Set your timer for thirty seconds, and then give an answer without looking at the timer. When your time is up, stop talking. Think back to how much you were able to communicate. Were you able to get through the important part of your answer?

If you were, keep practicing until you have a pretty good feel for what it means to give a thirty-second answer. Then, during the interview itself, use this as a guideline. Thirty seconds isn't very long, but if you end up talking a bit longer during an interview, you'll still manage to stop yourself at less than a minute.

If you aren't able to communicate the most important parts of your answers in thirty seconds, you'll need to practice boiling down your message. To do this, record yourself giving answers to a few common interview questions. Then listen to your answers and write down what you said in bullet points (i.e., not a word-for-word transcription). When you're done, look at your bullet points and circle just the most important point. Cross off any bullet points that aren't necessary for explaining that most important point. Now practice your answer out loud by talking only about the bullet points that you haven't crossed off. Working through several interview questions in this way should help you get a sense of the parts of your answers that you need to communicate during the interview, and which parts should be left for the first day at your new job.

If we did this for Brittany's full answer (not all of which was quoted above), it would look something like this:

- ~~The testing company is in a town that is a hub for educational testing~~
- ~~Some of her family lives in Iowa City; they like seeing her~~
- ~~She spends summers in Iowa City~~
- ~~She had a dining job she didn't like~~
- ~~The company hires people for temp jobs; most are retired professors~~
- She was a temp scorer, scoring math exams
- She was asked to join a special project
- ~~The president of the company loves Ann Arbor and joked with her about it~~
- The special project was to redesign a test
- The company was investigating how to be flexible with the language its test-takers use in their answers to better accommodate differences unrelated to math ability
- **Her job was to interpret the sentence structure** ←*Most important point*
- She was good at it
- She worked harder than normal
- ~~The test gives teachers and principals feedback on areas in which students score poorly so that they can focus on teaching those areas~~
- ~~Teachers in some schools skip over lessons or entire chapters~~

- ~~There are test tutors, but not everyone knows about them~~
- She was interested in the project and loved the work
- ~~The company was great to work for, with smart people and good policies~~

With this reduced list of topics, her answer ought to now be less than half as long. Brittany doesn't need to go down the path of describing a job she didn't like, and she might find herself focusing more on what *she* did on the job and spending less time on what the company did. She might even have time to add a more important point that she left out of her original answer, how she might apply skills learned in her last internship to a future internship in international trade.

Of course, regardless of your tendencies, you can always talk for less than thirty seconds or a minute when you answer simple questions. Also, thirty seconds isn't a hard and fast rule. Some answers really do need to be longer. Practicing with the thirty-second mark just gives you a way to stop yourself from continuing to talk so that you can hear and respond to the next question.

HOW TO TELL WHEN YOU'VE SAID ENOUGH

Sometimes, people keep talking because they don't have a very good sense of whether they have answered a question fully. The interviewer may not want to interrupt, and so may let you go on and on. Don't assume your interviewer will stop you; you need to be able to stop yourself.

If you need a way to trigger yourself to stop talking, try ending your answers with an open-ended question like, "Does that make sense?" or "Does anyone need more clarity about my answer?" or "I can elaborate more on that if you would like." This allows you to indicate that you think your answer is complete, but also that you understand that your interviewer may want more information. This is a way to turn the conversation back to them without being abrupt.

This technique is especially handy when you find yourself in a structured interview. A fully structured interview is one in which the interviewer must ask a predetermined list of questions and is not supposed to deviate from the list. When you end your answer by asking whether the interviewer needs more information, this allows the interviewer to take a little leeway if they are so inclined. Instead of rushing on to the next question, they can ask for a more complete answer in case you didn't provide sufficient detail.

ANSWERS THAT ARE TOO SHORT

The converse rule is that you also want to avoid answers that are too brief. You need to give the interviewer enough information to evaluate your candidacy.

Interviewers sometimes word their questions as if they might be answered with a simple yes or no. Quick agreement is okay for some questions ("Are you over the age of 18?"), but for other questions, you will need to learn to recognize that the interviewer is really inviting you to provide more information than they are literally asking for.

For instance, if an interviewer asks, "Have you used Excel before?" you'll want to say more than yes or no. You could say, "Yes, I have used Excel in several class projects, including making predictive models of bond prices and creating figures to present results of a research study." This simple elaboration accomplishes several things. It provides evidence to support your claim that you have used Excel, and it gives details about the types of things that you can use Excel to do when you start your new job.

If your answer is a negative ("No, I haven't used Excel"), you can also use elaboration in order to alleviate any strong concerns that answer might raise in the interviewer's mind. For instance, you could say:

> I haven't used Excel, but I have used the spreadsheets feature in
> Google Docs, which uses very similar formulas to those in

Excel. I'm confident that I could learn Excel quickly given what I know about how spreadsheets work.

BE SPECIFIC

Although we don't advise you to be long-winded, or to include details that are irrelevant to your story, there is utility in making your answers specific. This is another reason not to make your answers too short. A vague answer, even if it is brief and to the point, is often not a compelling answer. The following answer to the question "Tell me about your biggest accomplishment," for instance, is too short:

> In one of my toughest classes, I got an A+. I was one of the best students in the class.

In contrast, an answer that is more specific and contains a few more details makes the story more engaging and approachable. The interviewer should be able to picture this situation, even feel the experience along with you:

> On the first day of my organic chemistry class, the professor let us know that he grades on a curve. In a class our size, only two students earn an A+. I was determined to be one of those students. I studied really hard and attended office hours whenever I could. By the end of the semester, I knew I had done well, but I wasn't sure how my grade on the final exam compared to those of other students. The day grades were due to be posted, I logged in as soon as I woke up. I got the A+, and it was such a good feeling to know that I had earned it. I was so happy, I yelled something silly like "Woohoo!" and woke up my roommates by accident. They got over it though, when I bought them a beer that night to celebrate.

Which of these versions leaves you feeling excited for the job candidate? Which might you remember longer? Which would make you feel like you knew where the candidate was coming from, and what their motivations were? The specific details make the second version much better than the first. If you can add detail without talking for too long or describing things that confuse the interviewer or distract from your story, this will make your answers and your story more interesting.

BOXING YOURSELF INTO A CORNER

Interviewers will take you at your word. If you answer questions in a way that seems definitive, they will assume there is no additional complexity to the matter. For this reason, we recommend that you avoid sounding extreme, unless you specifically mean to be definitive. In other words, try not to box yourself into a corner. If you're asked, "Do you work well on your own?" it's often best not to say, "I really prefer working with other people."

If it's true that you have a very strong preference to work with others (perhaps you're an extreme extrovert, and you hate being by yourself), then of course you can say it. (After all, one of the principles to communicate is that you are speaking accurately.) If you are firmly against working alone, you *want* employers to use this information to disqualify you from jobs that you would hate, jobs that wouldn't supply you with enough social interaction. A job with no social interaction would not be the right fit for you, and you have no reason to vie for that job offer.

But if you look closely, our example answer didn't actually answer the question that was asked. It communicated important information to the interviewer, just not the information that the interviewer was looking for. What the interviewer wanted to know was, *if I give this person a project to do alone, will it get done?* If you're capable of doing great work on your own, but you prefer working with others, a better answer would be something like this:

> Yes, I'm very effective working on my own. For instance, during my senior year independent study, I only had three meetings with my professor; most of my time in that class was spent researching and writing a paper on the expansion of solar power

in the US. I'm curious, how much of my time spent here would involve working independently and how much would you expect me to be working with others?

This answer provides the interviewer with an accurate answer to their question. And even better, by following it up with a question of your own, you can gain insight about the position to help you decide whether it's the right fit.

USE THE EVIDENCE AT HAND

In the last chapter we recommended practicing your answers out loud with a partner or on video. If you use one of these strategies, your practice sessions can also teach you about your verbal and physical tendencies and whether you're managing to act professionally throughout the whole process. Once you feel comfortable with your ability to incorporate your story into your answers, consider investigating whether:

- Your answers get lost because you get off track or ramble;
- You speak too quietly; or
- You have a tendency to mumble or let your sentences trail off.

We recommend paying attention to these few things because they can make the interviewing process harder for the interviewer. When the interviewer struggles to hear you, to discern the message you meant to convey, or to figure out whether or not you're done talking, it takes their focus away from evaluating whether you're a great candidate.

That said, please don't waste your time on performance-related aspects of your interview practice sessions if you haven't already mastered the art of communicating your main points. We also don't recommend spending much time critiquing your body language or how many times you say "um." In reality, hardly anyone uses gestures so much or so little that they become distracting. But if you're confident that your answers are solid and that your physical and verbal tics are the only parts of your interview that need improvement, then feel free to start learning how to improve them.

TAKE YOUR TIME

You may find that some questions are very easy to answer. They may be questions that came up during your practice sessions, or questions that are fact-based like, "How long did you work in this position?" You can answer these questions naturally.

Other questions will be more difficult. Don't feel like you need to answer these questions as soon as the interviewer has stopped speaking. Be thoughtful and take a moment to recall what you learned during your practice sessions. Think about your story and what it is that you are trying to communicate. Think about the examples and experiences that are best suited to answering the question you've been asked. If the answer requires a narrative, take the time to think about where to start. Set up the necessary background, but don't go into irrelevant details. Above all, don't panic if there are a few seconds of silence as you prepare your answer.

And finally, if you're really stumped, talk to the interviewer about it. Ask for clarification, or admit that you've never been in a situation like the one they asked about. You might ask to revisit the question later, if something comes to mind as the interview continues.

STAY ON MESSAGE

By now, you've separated the good segments from the not-so-good segments of your work and educational history. You know the key accomplishments you want to describe as well as which parts of your work history are not really related to the job at hand. A good interviewer will ask you questions that make it easy to communicate your story without going into extraneous details. If you find yourself in a straightforward interview with good questions, your main job (beyond delivering the content) is to keep your answers brief and informative.

Nevertheless, in rare circumstances you may encounter an interviewer who asks questions that aren't about your education, work history, skills, personality, or any of the other components of your story. You might be

122

asked, "If you could have dinner with any three people—alive or dead—who would they be?" or "If you could be any animal, what would you be?" These questions are often asked to try to lower your guard, to see how you deal with novel situations, or as a (very weak) measure of your personality.

If you find yourself in the midst of this type of interview, your job is to *stay on message*. Answer the interviewer's questions in the context of who you are as a worker, not who you are as a human being. For example, if a job seeker wants to communicate that they are a very careful and deliberate employee, they might say, "If I could be any animal, I'd be a three-toed sloth, because they don't rush into situations too fast."

A job seeker who doesn't stay on message might answer, "I'd be a horse because I've always loved horses." This answer doesn't communicate anything about who they would be in the office, and it therefore doesn't help their cause. You should always answer questions honestly—if the interviewer does ask literally about your *favorite* animal, horse might be the right answer. But if you have wiggle room, you should use it to communicate your story.

SUMMARY

- Keep your answers relatively brief and focused on relevant information. Practice your timing if brevity is difficult for you.
- Details help your interviewer to remember your answer, as long as they are on point and brief.
- Communicate strong preferences only if you want them to be used to exclude you from certain jobs.
- Use practice to focus on the content that you want communicated; your body language and vocal expression are not as important as what you say.
- Keep revisiting the elements of your story, even when the interview questions seem unrelated to work.

CHAPTER 13: EVALUATE THE ORGANIZATION

In the middle of their mock interview, Charles asked Jessica for the most challenging or frustrating thing about her current job. Jessica, who is a very friendly and bubbly person, remarked that there wasn't anything frustrating about her job because she worked at a spa and her customers were always happy. She wrapped up her answer by comparing this situation to her last job, at a big box office supply retailer. Intrigued by the comparison, Charles asked about that previous experience. Jessica told him, "The customers get really upset sometimes, like really angry." According to Jessica, many customers had problems with the products, certain company policies were unethical, and its employees weren't treated well. After describing these experiences, she said, "It was a great comparison. Now I know what a real job that cares is like, and I know what a job that doesn't care is like." In the future, Jessica might evaluate the reputation of the organization and learn about its policies before accepting a job.

One of your two responsibilities during the interview is to figure out whether you really do want the job. (The other responsibility is to make the interviewer feel comfortable hiring you, and you've been working on that one for the last several chapters.) Regardless of how much you already know about the organization, the people who work there, and the job itself, you can always learn more. Unfortunately, you'll never know

124

with absolute certainty if the job and the organization are a perfect fit for you before you start working there. But taking the time to evaluate whether you might be satisfied and happy in an organization and in a specific job will weed out a lot of bad experiences like the one that Jessica described above.

RESEARCH STARTS EARLY

Ideally, researching an organization should begin before you apply for a job. But whenever you start the process—before deciding to apply, while targeting your resume to the job, before your interview, or after it—there are many good ways to learn about an organization.

READ THE JOB AD

There is often a section at the beginning or end of the job ad that describes the company and its employees. It may say things like "Fast-paced start-up is looking for…"; this communicates that they're looking for an employee who will work hard and be comfortable with change. Or it could say, "We're a Fortune 500 company…" in order to let you know that they are a very big company with a lot of revenue.

READ THE ORGANIZATION'S WEBSITE

You don't have to read its entire website, but certain pages may be very useful in finding details about an organization, especially one you're not very familiar with. The website should be useful for answering questions like:

- How is the organization structured? Is it for-profit or nonprofit, publically traded or private, run by a single person, a small partnership, a family, or a cooperative?

- How does the organization earn money? Who gives money to whom? Which functional units make money, and which seem like they might cost more money than they bring in?
- Who are the senior managers or leaders? Who are the managers and coworkers you might have daily interactions with? What are the backgrounds of these people? Do you seem to have things in common with them?
- What is the history of the organization? How old is it? Has it been growing, staying the same size over time, or getting smaller?
- What recent achievements has the organization made? What are the current projects you might end up working on?

SEARCH FOR MORE DETAILS

Do an internet search for the name of the organization. Make sure you look past the first page of results in order to determine what the media, financial analysts, and competitors are saying about it. When possible, seek out the organization's financial statements. If you can, compare statements over the past few years. Is revenue or profit declining over time? If so, can you figure out a good reason, or might the health of the organization be in question? If the organization is publicly traded, how has its stock price been moving relative to competitors or the market in general? You might also find interesting information from a Google News search.

SEEK OUT OTHER PERSPECTIVES

Use social media, blogs, and forums to learn what others think about the organization. Are reviews from past employees generally positive or negative? Do clients or customers seem satisfied with the products or services they receive? If you have a connection to someone who works at the organization, get their perspective as well. They may be able to help you put what you've learned from other sources into context.

RESEARCH LEADING UP TO THE INTERVIEW

The impression of the organization that you developed through the initial research that we've described above should continue to develop as you are contacted to set up an interview. Is the process for scheduling casual (done by a chatty email or phone call) or is it more formal and bureaucratic (with a letter mailed to your home)? Do the people you talk to sound friendly? Do they sound like they know what they're doing or are they struggling to figure out how to schedule your interview?

RESEARCH DURING THE INTERVIEW

When you arrive for the interview, you will have even more information to gather. What are people wearing? If you're invited back for a second interview, should you increase or decrease the formality of your clothing to match their look? Are people running from room to room hectically, walking at a normal pace, or meandering as if they have no need or desire to arrive at their destination? If you walk through a workspace to get to the interview room, is there much background noise? (Will you be able to get work done in a place where everyone whispers, where there are side conversations going on all the time, or where there are frequent loud disagreements?)

At some point during the interview, the interviewer will likely take a few minutes to give you more details about the job. This might include a description of the tasks or projects you will work on, who you will work with, or what the organization is like. Pay careful attention to what is said, and take notes on any key facts that you think you might forget before this potentially stressful day is over.

Here are some questions you may want to ask yourself as you learn more about the organization:

- Is your future manager someone you can learn from? Do you think they will be interested in facilitating your career development?

- Are you getting consistent impressions of the company culture, or does the stated culture (as it appears on the company website or in the job ad) differ from what you're seeing and hearing from the interviewer?
- Do you think you would get along with your potential coworkers?
- If you have more than one interviewer, do they seem to get along, or at least respect each other?
- Does the work environment seem like a place where you might be productive?
- Would you have a chance to use the skills and knowledge that you hope to use?
- Is this job a good fit for your desired career path?
- Would you enjoy doing the work as you understand it?
- Do you think you would be able to meet or exceed the expectations and benchmarks for this job?

Keep in mind, one great way to find the answers to these questions is to ask.

COME PREPARED WITH QUESTIONS

In order to ask questions of the interviewer that are specific to your needs and that will give you useful information, think about what you want to know and how to ask about it ahead of time. Write your questions down in a prioritized list (from most important to least important) and take them with you to the interview. A prioritized list will come in handy if you don't have time to ask every question. You can always ask more questions in subsequent interviews, or after you've been offered the job but before you accept it. But it's nice to have answers to your most pressing questions so that you can decide whether or not you want to move on to the next phase of the job search.

One of the most important things to learn before the interview is who will interview you. This doesn't mean you have to know where they went to school and the names of their pets (creepy!). It does mean that, at a minimum, you should know what they do at the company. Are you interviewing with people who you would manage, who would be your peers, who would be your boss, or with someone who is even higher up in the hierarchy? Are you interviewing with people you would work with on a daily basis, or are they just decision makers whom you wouldn't interact with? Who has hiring authority? You can usually find all of this out by asking the person who schedules your interview.

Having this information will help you to ask the right questions of the right people. Below, we walk you through a few examples of the types of questions you might ask and to whom you might ask these questions. The point is to ask questions of people who know the answers, not people who might have to guess. If someone can't give you the information you're looking for, ask them something else. For example, if you want to know how long employees typically stay at the company, you *could* ask anyone about the organization's turnover rate. But a representative from human resources is the person who is most likely to give you the most accurate answer. Other people could probably give you an estimate, but that estimate may be skewed toward those people's experiences. In other words, those answers will be based on smaller samples, like the employees in their team or in their department or the number of people who have left since they themselves were hired.

When talking to a human resources professional, ask questions about:

- Dress code (before the in-person interview)
- Responsibilities and duties
- Professional development and training opportunities
- Employee turnover rates
- Compensation and benefits (preferably not at the first interview, ideally you should try to wait until a job offer negotiation)
- Performance evaluation schedules and metrics

When interviewing with the hiring manager, ask questions about:

- Timeline for the hiring process
- Expectations for the new hire and traits sought
- That person's management style
- Requirements for or likelihood of advancement
- Duties and assignments

When talking to peers, ask questions about:

- Their impressions of management (but only if their boss isn't in the room!)

Anyone in the organization can provide you with details about:

- Organizational culture
- Their specific role in the organization
- Their career trajectory (e.g., how long they've been there, their promotion history)
- Their likes and dislikes about the organization
- Previous or upcoming changes in the organization (e.g., growth, restructuring)
- Industry-related questions and comparisons to competitor organizations

Do *not* ask about these topics—with anyone:

- Facts that can be found on the company's website or through a quick internet search
- Gossip about coworkers or the company

One other note about your questions: they should be genuine. That is, you should honestly want to know the answers to these questions. Ideally, those answers will give you insight into whether you want to work in the job and for the organization.

LISTEN TO CLUES

Just as your questions will reflect what you want to know about the job and the organization, the interviewer's questions will give you a sense of what topics are important to them. Their questions—especially behavioral and situational ones—can be good clues as to the types of situations and tasks that you will encounter on the job. If you're asked several questions about conflict—how you might handle conflict with customers, coworkers, and managers, for instance—you can expect to experience conflict in the job. The interviewer is giving you a hint that previous employees have experienced or created conflict in the past. If conflict makes you uncomfortable, you may want to seek clarification about this aspect of the position before accepting an offer. Similarly, if you're asked about skills that weren't mentioned in the job ad, the tasks that you encounter may not be the ones you are expecting.

SUMMARY

- One of the two most important things to do during an interview is to figure out whether you want the job.
- Start your research of the organization early, and continue to evaluate the organization throughout your interactions with employees.
- Be ready to ask your own questions during the interview, and be sure that you're asking questions that are best answered by the person you're speaking with.
- Listen for hints about what you may encounter in the job by paying attention to the topics that the interviewer brings up.

You've articulated your strengths, you've learned to tell your story, and you've practiced to become your very best. Now what?

Even though you've gotten much better at interviewing by learning how to communicate your story, you probably won't deliver a knockout performance in every interview. The truth is that there is always room to get better, and there is one thing in particular you can do to get even better at interviewing. Evaluate how the interview went and think about your perceptions of the organization *before* they give you a job offer.

WHY BOTHER THINKING ABOUT SOMETHING THAT JUST HAPPENED?

People have a tendency to believe that any given outcome was inevitable once it has happened, even if they didn't know what the outcome would be before it happened. If you wait until you hear that an organization is not interested in hiring you, you may think that you knew this was going to happen all along. When you think back on the interview after having been turned down, it will inevitably seem like it went poorly. You may blame yourself, the interviewer (perhaps they didn't ask you the right questions), or someone else (perhaps there are many overqualified job seekers in your area, and they're taking all the entry-level jobs that should be given to younger people). Your memories will have faded and you'll think back on only the negative aspects of the interview.

Alternatively, what if you're offered the job? It's tempting to believe that this means that your interviewing skills are absolutely amazing and you couldn't have done any better. You might feel that you don't even need to practice the next time you decide to look for a job. After all, you're a master, and getting future jobs will be as easy as showing up to interview on the scheduled day. (We hope you can read our sarcasm.)

Putting an interview experience out of mind as soon as you walk out the door can also lead you to make the wrong decision about accepting the job. If you're presented with a strong job offer, you may find yourself deciding that you really like the organization. Perhaps the hiring manager said a lot of great things about you when they called with the offer; maybe they talked up all of the benefits you would receive if you worked there. If you have received an offer without already deciding whether the organization is right for you, it will be really difficult to objectively evaluate their offer. That decision is too important to let someone make for you.

And if you're still not convinced that you need to reflect on your job interview, do it for another reason. If nothing else, writing down the questions that you answered well, or the questions that you didn't address particularly well, gives you great content for a thank you letter.

For all of these reasons, it's best to evaluate the interview experience before you learn its outcome. It is very important to *write down* your perceptions so you don't forget them later. With written notes, you'll have an objective impression of how the interview went that you can then use to improve your interview skills in the future as well as to decide whether you want to accept a job offer.

As soon as you have a moment to yourself after the interview is over, think about your overall impressions.

Then think about the interview in chronological order, stopping at each memorable event (walking into the office, shaking hands, greeting your interviewer, and so forth) and again at each interview question that you can remember. Evaluate each of these in your mind and then compose written notes.

After thinking about the interview by yourself, talk about the experience with several people. Ideally, these should be people who will ask you a lot of questions. Conversation will help you to reflect on things that may have escaped your attention. For instance, a friend might ask if people were smiling in the office. If you talk about this on the same day that you had the interview, you'll be able to remember whether you saw people who seemed to be happy to be at their jobs. If you try to remember this next month when you're evaluating the job offer, your recollection won't be as accurate.

Next, jot down what you learned about the company. What are the expectations that were communicated to you? What did you learn about the company culture? Were they asking questions that focused on specific tasks or skills? If so, these will probably be key to your success on the job.

Finally, think through the highlights, lowlights, and what you plan to do in future interviews. To help you along in this process of evaluating your interview, we've created an Interview Evaluation Guide.

INTERVIEW EVALUATION GUIDE

Overview

- How well prepared did you feel walking into the interview?
- Which questions surprised you or caught you off guard?

The positives

- Which of your answers best communicated your story? What worked about those answers?

The negatives

- Which of your answers did not communicate your story very well? Why did they fall short? (Perhaps your answer didn't fit with the rest of your story or was confusing. Maybe you just couldn't think of an answer.)

The company

- Did you get a clear sense of what you would do on a daily basis?
- Do you know who you would work with? Who would you report to? Who would you interact with on a daily basis? Who would you interact with only occasionally?
- Do you think you could get along reasonably well with the people you met? (Include everyone you interacted with, not just the interviewers.)
- Do you think this position will allow you to use your skills and knowledge and help you meet your career goals?
- Do you know what will be expected of you, how you will be evaluated, and what you will need to do to excel in this position?
- Are you excited about the possibility of working for this organization and with these people?

For the future

- What might you do differently during your next interview?

DISLIKING AN ORGANIZATION

If you don't like to fail, you may find yourself writing something like, "I don't think I liked this organization." That way, you'll be able to soothe your ego if they don't extend you an offer. You'll just say to yourself, *that job would have been awful—I'm glad they didn't bother calling me back!*

It's fine to write down negative opinions if they are in fact true. But try to avoid being pre-emptively negative in order to save your feelings. This is a little like breaking up with someone just so they don't break up with you first. Why not give it a little time? It's okay to like a job or an organization even if you're not exactly the right fit, right now. That doesn't mean you'll never get to work there. In fact, a better position may open up in the future, or your future work experiences may make you a more desirable candidate.

If you evaluate an organization negatively just to feel better about rejection in the future, you'll also be less likely to be happy or satisfied with the job offer when it does come. You'll look back at your written reflections and think, *oh, but I didn't like this organization. Maybe I shouldn't accept the offer.*

If you're always evaluating jobs or organizations negatively and you know that it's not because you're afraid of rejection, you may be applying to the wrong jobs. In this case, it's time to do more research about organizations before you bother applying and going on interviews and to honestly evaluate whether this is indeed the field you want to work in. For instance, if you find yourself frustrated that every banking job in New York City requires ridiculous hours, perhaps you need to consider living in a different area or working for a less prestigious firm where the expectations may be a little lower.

SUCCESS IS NOT MEASURED IN JOB OFFERS

You should always remember that whether or not you get a job offer shouldn't define how well the interview went. You can make a great impression in the mind of an interviewer and still not be the best fit for the job. If you are considering a job offer and reflecting on the interview, keep in mind that the cost of a bad fit is high for both you and your employer. If you don't think you can deliver what the job requires, it may be best for you to pass on the offer. And instead of thinking about whether you aced an interview, instead of letting the outcome dictate how you feel about the process, you can define for yourself whether or not the interview was a success. If you can remember this while you're in the interview itself, it will help you be more objective and less nervous. It will also help you to stay positive throughout the whole job search process.

SUMMARY

- If you receive a job offer, your earlier evaluation of your interview will prepare you to decide whether you want to accept it.
- Evaluations should ideally include time that you spend thinking about the interview by yourself, and time that you spend talking about the interview to other people.
- Write down your evaluation. This will help you to remember its most important points, especially if you're going on multiple interviews at multiple organizations, or if the hiring process drags on for several weeks.

CHAPTER 15: THE ADVANCED LESSON

After having worked through the previous chapters, you'll be more prepared than other job candidates for the interview process. You can stop here if you like.

Or, you can read this chapter, and learn how to wow your interviewer.

Good job candidates know that they need to talk up their strengths, highlight their value to the organization, convey their interest in the job, and come across as a professional who will fit in. But the very best job candidates go even further. They embody that old adage about writing: show, don't tell. Instead of simply talking about their ability to do the job well and how great they would be in the position, they *show* the interviewer that this is true by answering questions thoughtfully and with integrity. In this chapter, we'll describe how to show off your best qualities in just this way.

DESCRIBING YOURSELF

An interview will often start with some version of "Tell me about yourself" or "Walk me through your resume." You may come across advice that says these are throwaway questions used by interviewers to help you get comfortable. These questions are certainly intended that way by some interviewers, and they're viewed that way by many job seekers, like Andrew. When Charles asked Andrew to tell him a bit about himself at the beginning of their mock interview, Andrew responded:

> I'm a student at the University of Michigan, grew up in Michigan most of my life. So some of the things I like to do personally—spending time with family, traveling, that's just, the very personal side. Love music, play the piano, love creating music, listening to music. That's basically me in a nutshell.

Andrew's answer would have been great if he had been interviewing for a job as a pianist. As a would-be business consultant, he missed a chance to make a case for himself. You can use this question much more effectively.

If you get this kind of opener, it is the *perfect* opportunity to provide the outline of your story because it's the only time you can say whatever you want about yourself. (The rest of the interview is going to be spent responding to more specific questions.) Tell the interviewer the highlights of your story that you are certain you need to communicate. When you revisit these points later in the interview, the interviewer will recall that you've already said something similar. This reinforcement of your core message will help to confirm that message for the interviewer.

Good answers to questions like these usually convey at least some of the following: the job seeker's educational background, why the job seeker is a great fit for the position, and the fact that the job seeker actually wants this position. For instance, a candidate might say:

> I attended Arizona State University. While I was there, I volunteered at a nonprofit where I tutored elementary school students in math and science. I loved working with kids of all different cultural backgrounds; I feel like I learned as much from the kids as they learned from me. It was such a great fit that I'm looking for a job in which I can build on that volunteer experience. I want to make a difference in the lives of underprivileged youth.

If there are any obvious red flags on your resume that you can effectively talk about, feel free to bring them up as well. That way, you can control the way they are discussed, and you won't have to worry about whether or not the interviewer has interpreted your situation appropriately:

> I attended Arizona State University. I realized that college wasn't a great fit for me right now, because I was becoming overwhelmed by my growing student loan debt. I decided it would be better for me to get a job and start paying down some of the debt. Eventually, I may decide to save up and go back to get my degree when I can pay for it.
>
> Luckily, while I was in school I also volunteered...

You can also add a little about your interests or life outside work, like Andrew did. The introductory question is a good time to mention activities or hobbies that may be similar to those of other employees, which allows you to show that you would fit well in the organization. Charles followed up his initial question by asking about Andrew's interest in traveling, and they were able to bond over the fact that both of them had recently spent time on Cape Cod. The key is to not *only* talk about life outside work. Stick mostly to your story and to the elements of your story that you most need to share with the interviewer.

As with your answers to other questions, you'll want to practice answering this type of introductory question. It can be tempting to try to memorize your answer because these questions are so common. *Do not* memorize your answer. You want to sound professional and clear, but you don't want to sound like you're reading. A stilted answer will make the interviewer think they are getting a scripted and hence potentially fake version of who you are instead of an accurate and honest depiction.

COMMUNICATING PERSONAL QUALITIES

There are many soft skills that interviewers, and people in general, find endearing. By soft skills, we mean qualities that are rarely mentioned in job ads, but which can make the difference between a good employee and a great one. Good interviewers will be pleasantly surprised to find someone with these traits among their pool of job candidates.

Below, we discuss a few of these qualities and describe how you might demonstrate them during your interviews. If you don't think a particular trait describes you, then don't try to communicate that quality as you frame your answers. Our examples are mostly meant to show you how to think about your discussion with the interviewer, as well as how to demonstrate the ways in which you embody characteristics that help people to succeed in professional life. So if you feel like the traits we've highlighted in this chapter don't describe you well, think of other ones that do and what it would take to exhibit them in an interview. Doing so will make you stand out from the crowd.

SHOWING POSITIVITY

People like coworkers who are able to maintain positive (or at least balanced) attitudes on most days. This doesn't mean that you need to fake being cheery on your worst days. It doesn't mean that you should only say positive things, or that you can't talk about negative experiences. Being positive means that when you do talk about negative things, you don't dwell on them and let them bring you down. If you find yourself answering a question about a negative experience or quality, you can always bring your answer back to a positive light.

Consider this negative answer to the question "How do you handle criticism?":

> Ugh, I hate criticism so much. It's so frustrating to try to do a good job and then someone just tears you apart for it. In my last job, there was another waiter who was constantly criticizing me. One time when he said, "Oh, you didn't mention your name when you greeted that table," it was the last straw. I told him to mind his own business, and he got all defensive, like, "I'm just trying to give you advice to increase your tips!" I swear, I wanted to punch him.

It's probably clear to the interviewer that this job seeker does not handle criticism well. And hey, if you don't handle criticism well and you want to fess up to that weakness, that's fine. But you don't have to do it in such an overwhelming way. Instead, try to stay positive. A good way to do this is to talk about improvements from your past—even if they are small. What have you learned? How have you gotten better? Focus on staying positive during the interview, and demonstrate that you can bring that mindset into the workplace.

A better answer to a question about criticism would be:

> I'm not very good at handling criticism. In fact, if you were to ask me about a weakness, dealing with criticism would probably be it. In the past, I tended to overgeneralize criticism and hear it as a critique of me as a person instead of a critique of something I have done. Recently, I have started dealing with it by taking a step back and realizing that most times, the person criticizing me is trying to help me perform at a higher level. I'd like to work with my next manager to try to find ways to keep getting better at taking criticism because I know that constructive criticism is important for self-improvement.

Note that in the more positive answer, the job seeker doesn't go into detail explaining an overreaction in the past because the focus is on improvements and plans for the future.

DISPLAYING RESPECTFULNESS

Did your parents ever say, "Don't say things about people that you wouldn't say to their face"? They were right. This is especially true when you're trying to impress someone who has the authority to hire you. If a job candidate makes disparaging remarks about people who have hired her, trained her, or tried to help her learn in school or in the workplace, it makes her seem ungrateful and disrespectful. For example, if the interviewer asks a job seeker to describe the most difficult person she ever had to work with, the following answer would be disrespectful:

My boss at my work-study job was unbearable. He had an awful sense of humor. When he made jokes and I rolled my eyes at him, he'd make a big deal about how everyone else thought he was funny and I didn't. He also had a very nit-picky way he wanted everything done; he was such a micromanager. We really didn't see eye-to-eye on anything. And his breath smelled so bad! I was so glad when that semester was over and I never had to work with him again!

An interviewer might be able to relate to the emotions and difficult situations expressed in this answer. But even if it's possible to relate to this answer, the job seeker comes across as complaining about someone for whom she should have had respect. A bad boss might still be a good person; who wants to work with someone who disparages others?

A better answer would focus not on criticizing the boss's humor or breath, but instead focus on why that boss was difficult to work with:

I had a hard time learning to work with my boss at my work-study job. He had been managing students a long time, over thirty years, and had developed a very particular method of getting the job done that he made everyone adhere to. It's understandable—he had so many years dealing with students who hadn't had much work experience before—but I felt like he wasn't open to trying to increase efficiency. I tried showing him that switching the order of document processing would save time, but he wasn't willing to listen to my ideas or change the way things were done. It was frustrating, but I ended up learning a lot about how to stay motivated while working within an established system.

Note that in the more respectful answer, the job seeker doesn't complain about things that are not work-related. Instead, her answer focuses on the frustrating experience of having good ideas and not having those ideas adopted, or even heard. It also shows that she thought about her boss's point of view and why he was doing things this particular way. This shows respect, even when their viewpoints differ.

WHEN THE BEST DEFENSE IS NOT A GOOD OFFENSE

If you're trying to demonstrate respectfulness, here's another tip: be mindful of things that can be offensive. Your interviewer is likely a stranger whose life history, opinions, and viewpoints are unknown to you. Despite what you may see as commonalities between the two of you, or even what is common in your local area, it's best to avoid sensitive topics. Stay away from discussing controversial news or elections (unless you're interviewing for a job in politics, of course). And be careful when using humor.

Words describing people can be particularly loaded. If you think you will need to talk about groups of people—especially people who are different from you—and you aren't sure how to do it, take the opportunity to learn how to do this. Most professors are up-to-date on preferred terminology. If you aren't in touch with professors who can help you, simply look online. The website of the organization you've applied to may have text describing the populations of people with whom you would be working; try mirroring their language. Otherwise, it's best to avoid these sensitive topics altogether.

REMAINING OPEN

Interviewers like to feel that candidates are open about themselves and their interest in the position. An open job seeker comes across as someone whom the interviewer can get to know. Discussing things like your worst work experiences with a complete stranger can be awkward. But if you don't answer honestly, you will sound evasive. Things that make job seekers sound evasive and closed-off include curt responses, vague responses, and the active avoidance of questions. For instance, none of these responses to the prompt "Tell me about an obstacle you have had to overcome" are open enough:

> I had a hard time in school. [The interviewer is thinking, *do you have a learning disability, or were you bullied, or unmotivated, or what?*]

I don't really feel comfortable talking about my biggest obstacle. [Then why not talk about a different obstacle?]

Well, there's a big speed bump on my street that I have to drive over at least twice a day. Ha ha. [Beware of using humor to avoid answering a question; it will be apparent that you didn't mention a real obstacle.]

One of the biggest problems with these evasive-sounding answers is that some interviewers will sense that the job seeker is putting up their defenses and will want to respect their boundaries. When this happens, the interviewer will move on to the next question rather than asking the job seeker follow-up questions to try to gather more information.

As an alternative, try to be open. In this example, the job seeker manages to talk successfully about a painful experience.

Doing well in high school was really hard for me because I moved three times. Each time was to a new school district in the middle of the school year. I had a hard time catching up to the other students. The last time we moved, when I was in eleventh grade, some of my teachers realized that it might be hard for me to join a school in December. One put me in a group with friendly students who didn't mind going over what they'd already learned, and another one agreed to tutor me after school twice a week. With their help and a lot of hard work, I graduated with a 3.8 GPA. I will always be grateful for the kindness and understanding they showed me.

For people who are not used to being open with strangers, this advice may be unsettling. Don't worry; you don't need to divulge your deepest secrets or tell the interviewer all of your hopes and dreams. The best way to be open during an interview is to focus on *facts*. The facts in the example above are things that the job seeker doesn't need to be ashamed of or insecure about. The facts are simply that the job seeker moved frequently, that it can be hard to catch up on course material in the middle of the school year, and that two teachers made this process easier.

The last sentence is a nice add-on because it demonstrates a capacity to be positive and gracious, but it's not necessary as part of an open answer.

Nowhere does this answer get overly personal, full of private opinions, or mired in the feelings of the job seeker. By focusing on facts, you can convey to the interviewer that they will be able to know you as you really are, why you do things, and what type of worker you will be.

DEMONSTRATING HONESTY

The word honesty rarely appears in job ads, but it is one of the key traits that employers look for in their employees. An honest employee is one who doesn't embezzle, doesn't steal proprietary information to start a new company, and doesn't get the organization into legal trouble by breaking government regulations. Luckily, these things don't happen all that often.

When employers want an honest employee, it's usually for more mundane reasons. Employers want to know that when problems arise, they will be addressed rather than buried. When it's time to evaluate performance, peer reviews are helpful and not used to sabotage coworkers. When new client relationships are being formed, employers need to know that the only promises being made are ones that can indeed be kept. These things are the backbone of organizations with strong reputations, and they are dependent on having honest employees.

How can you demonstrate your honesty during an interview? First, do not lie. Sometimes questions require direct answers. If someone asks you, "Are you the best programmer you know?" and you aren't, you should not lie and say you are.

Next, be willing to admit your mistakes. Nothing shows honesty like describing a time you made a bad decision, didn't get something done by the deadline, or let your emotions get the better of you. The best examples of these situations are ones in which you realized your mistake and fixed it, or when you genuinely learned from the mistake and can show that you'll be able to avoid that mistake in the future. If you share an example like this, the interviewer will know that you are honest, adaptable, and willing to work toward being the best person you can be.

One final way to demonstrate honesty is to be willing to acknowledge your shortcomings. The worst answer to "What is your biggest weakness?" is "I don't think I have any weaknesses." It's almost definitely a lie, and interviewers will take it as such. Instead, you can use this question as an opportunity to demonstrate that you are willing to be honest. Fessing up to your shortcomings shows the interviewer that you aren't trying to squeak by using half-truths.

Here is an example of a situation in which the job seeker isn't dishonest—there is no lying in the answer itself—but there is a missed opportunity to show genuine honesty:

> Interviewer: As you know, we have a lot of high-profile clients. Suppose you had an opportunity to meet a member of the royal family of Morocco as a representative of our company. What would you do?

> Job seeker: It would be a great honor to have that opportunity. I would strive to represent the company by being professional, courteous, and extremely well-informed about whatever projects the company wanted me to discuss.

There is nothing wrong with this answer, but the job seeker didn't use this chance to admit a shortcoming—that this assignment might be a stretch. In the following example, this is clearer:

> Job seeker: It would be a great honor to have that opportunity. To be honest, I'm sure there are formalities and customs that ought to be followed when meeting with Moroccan royalty, but I don't know what those are. The first thing I would do is read up on those customs, and ask the advice of anyone in the company who had done this type of thing in the past. Once I was better prepared, I would strive to represent the company by being professional, courteous, and extremely well-informed about whatever projects the company wanted me to discuss.

One of the ways job seekers lower their chances of being hired is by thinking that they need to have an answer—the correct answer—to every question. Sometimes the best answer is some version of "I don't know." Just don't stop there; a more complete answer will include describing how you might think about the problem, find an answer, or handle a similar situation.

TAKING RESPONSIBILITY

Employers absolutely want someone who takes responsibility for their role in a situation—whether the outcome is good or bad. One way to communicate that you are the type of person who takes responsibility is to make sure that the reasons you provide for prior bad outcomes don't focus solely on other people's failings. Some of the blame may indeed fall on other people's shoulders, but in most situations, you could have done something differently that might have changed the outcome.

After seeing a job seeker's transcript, an interviewer might ask, "Why did you have a D in one class when the rest of your grades were As and Bs?" Here's an answer that doesn't express personal responsibility:

> The teacher in that class was awful. I tried really hard to study the material, but there was too much to read and the class lectures were useless. Also, I could barely understand what the teacher was saying because of her thick accent.

An alternative answer still explains that the job seeker struggled to learn the material, but instead of blaming the teacher, this answer shows that the job candidate accepts personal responsibility for his academic performance and has identified strategies that could be useful in future situations that involve a heavy workload:

> I tried really hard to study the material, but I had a hard time keeping up with the large amount of required reading on top of my other classes and my part-time job. If I were to do that semester over again, I would have reduced the number of classes I was taking from five to four, and I would have tried to get

ahead in the reading assignments at the beginning of the semester, when I had less to do for my other classes.

You may have noticed that some of the examples from this chapter overlap. If you're being disrespectful, you probably also sound like you're not taking responsibility. If you aren't being open, you may also sound dishonest. In general, showing that you are a great employee because of one positive quality will convey that you have other positive qualities. It's easy to distinguish job candidates who are open, honest, respectful, *and* responsible from those who are the opposite.

If you think the traits we've highlighted in this chapter don't apply to you, think about ones that do. There is always room to grow and to continue to gain experiences that you can use to describe yourself in future interviews.

SUMMARY

- If you have the chance, start the interview by outlining the most important facts about you and your story.
- The best way to impress the interviewer is to frame your answers in a way that showcases the personal characteristics that will make you a great employee.
- Being honest and straightforward, while staying positive and emphasizing growth, is a great way to communicate difficult parts of your educational or work history. In contrast, being evasive makes the interviewer think you are hiding something, and that you will not be forthcoming if there are problems at work.

CHAPTER 16: MORE THAN ANSWERS

We haven't given you advice on every conceivable topic in the world of the job interview. We haven't told you exactly what to wear (hint: something at least as nice as what the organization's current employees wear), whether to send thank you notes (hint: yes) or how to negotiate an offer (hint: consider the employer's goals in addition to your own). If you want advice on these and other matters, you can find it—for free—on our website, morethananswers.com.

What we *have* given you is advice you won't hear anywhere else. We've learned to measure success not simply in the numbers of interviews our clients are able to garner, but by when they find and are offered positions that best utilize their skills and interests. And we know that job candidates are most successful not when they have an answer to every question, but when they learn to tell meaningful, accurate stories about their work lives.

We hope that you now understand how your education, your previous work history, and your other experiences can be combined to tell a story about who you are. You should have a general interview story that can be used as the basis for all of your upcoming job interviews. This story also functions as the kernel of an ongoing story that you will continue to expand and revise as you gain new experiences, pursue professional development, and grow as a worker and as a human being. Twenty years from now, your story may include a new turning point or some new interests, but it will still include elements of your story as it stands today.

You should also now have a more tailored version of your interview story that you can use in your next job interview. This adapted story shows how your unique combination of knowledge, skills, interests, and personal characteristics make you a great fit for this particular job, not just any job. You know exactly which pieces of your life story need to be told as parts of your interview story, and which pieces you can share later, when you're getting to know your new coworkers. Even better, you now have specific examples to help interviewers know that you're being accurate and honest.

Beyond knowing what to say, you should also have some sense of the communication pitfalls that trip up so many job seekers. You know what not to say: you want to describe experiences from which you've learned but you also want to provide your prospective employers with a good sense of *what* you've learned. You're aware of misperceptions people may have about you, and how to address them. You're ready to give clear and concise answers that allow you time to get through all of the interviewer's questions, so they have no lingering uncertainties about who you are.

Finally, we hope you also have a sense of how to portray your hidden qualities, the ones that are attractive to employers but that many job seekers don't know how to convey. As a result of the work that you've done here, you should be able to demonstrate that you're open, honest, positive, respectful, and can take responsibility as well as share credit for success.

Even when you're a qualified candidate who wants to work, it may take time to find a job. But you know that to be satisfied with the outcome of your job search, you need to be active. It's best to take the time not just to describe who you are in a way that makes sense, but also to learn about the organization and the job that's open. Finding a job that is the right fit for you is worth the effort.

All of these skills in communicating with potential employers proceed from the way you tell your story. With just a little bit of practice, you can learn not only to tell your story, but to tell it in ways that will help you find a job that speaks to your training, your interests, and most importantly, your heart. Good interview stories do more than answer questions; they communicate who you are.

Your next job is the next chapter of your story. The challenges you overcome and the skills you develop will lead you to future promotions and job opportunities. Success will come from living the story you want to tell.

About the Authors

Emily received a PhD in Education & Psychology at the University of Michigan, where her research focused on career development, educational decision-making, and career goals. After a post-doctoral fellowship, she returned to Ann Arbor to work at a non-profit, and later, to start More Than Answers, LLC with Charles.

Charles received an MSE in Industrial and Operations Engineering at the University of Michigan. He has worked for a company as a consultant, helping clients with technical problems, for 15 years, while also managing the business operations of the company. A life and career spent learning a little bit about a lot things helped him convincingly interview all of our wonderful participants in their vocation of choice. When he isn't playing basketball, he can usually be found watching, reading or otherwise obsessing about it.

If you have a question or a unique situation that isn't addressed in this book, or if you have any suggestions for improving our next edition, consider emailing us at emily@morethananswers.com.

And if you enjoyed this book, please check out the rest of our content on morethananswers.com. Let your friends know where they can find us. (We'd love a review on Amazon too!)

Made in the USA
Middletown, DE
11 December 2016